P9-CZV-436

I have to admit that I've battled a number of fierce "mind monsters" in my lifetime. Unfortunately, it *can* be hereditary. Habitual patterns of fear and anxiety that were rehearsed by previous generations (particularly my father and grandfather) now attempt to invade my own thinking from time to time.

Thankfully, Kevin Gerald has laid out for us concise, fundamental steps to setting up a border patrol capable of guarding our hearts and minds. Instantly, we're now able to recognize the enemy, reject the lies, replace the negative, and begin to retrain our thought patterns to form positive new habits. What a great blessing! This essential little book contains the secrets to defeating the mental attacks we encounter every day. It's so reassuring to know that we don't have to be afraid of monsters any more!

—DAVID CRANK
SENIOR PASTOR OF FAITH CHURCH ST. LOUIS

Pastor Gerald gives the practical and the powerful. His insights to the mind and its effect on our lives are motivating and inspiring. You will not only read the things that will help your life; you will also read how to make it happen. In a world of theories and good ideas, Pastor Gerald gives real substance that will change your life. *Mind Monsters* is one of the books that you will go back to again and again. Read it and go for it. You will overcome the "monsters" that have held you back.

—DR. CASEY TREAT
SENIOR PASTOR OF CHRISTIAN FAITH CHURCH
FEDERAL WAY, WA

Kevin Gerald has created an amazing guide to taking control of your thoughts and directing them in order to become the person you want to be. Using biblical principles, he will teach you how to stop negative thoughts from entering your mind and replace them with positive ones. *Mind Monsters* holds the key to unlocking the full potential of your mind and adopting a mentality of success that will propel you into greatness.

—Pastor Matthew Barnett
Cofounder of the Dream Center
Los Angeles, CA

If you are constantly battling negative thoughts and never seem to have a breakthrough in your thought processes, this book is for you. *Mind Monsters* is the key to unlock the mysteries of your thinking habits and help you walk out of the realm of negativity! Our thoughts form the framework of our entire being. The way we live life, act, talk, respond, and relate to people and the world around us is related to the way we think. In this book, Kevin Gerald guides the reader through a systematic approach to "take captive every thought to make it obedient to Christ." The reader who encounters this book will be irrevocably transformed for the better and will henceforth experience success in his daily walk as a Christian!

—Rev. Dr. Kong Hee
Pastor of City Harvest Church
Singapore

Without a doubt *Mind Monsters* should be required reading for every Christian. If we can learn to think right, everything else often follows. This is one of the best books on the subject of the mind I have read and one I personally have on my bookshelf and refer to frequently. Kevin Gerald has a profound ability to make God's Word practical and applicable to all of us. Don't think about reading this book—do it!

—Christine Caine
Director of Equip and Empower Ministries, and founder
of The A21 Campaign

Pastor Kevin Gerald is one the most gifted communicators in the church today. In his brilliant book *Mind Monsters*, he gives definition to the battles that rage in all our minds and provides practical strategies for taking back control and living victoriously. This book is rich in wisdom and insight. It's an essential tool in the hand of every believer and essential weaponry for every leader helping people fight "mind monsters."

—CHARLOTTE SCANLON-GAMBILL
SENIOR ASSOCIATE PASTOR OF ABUNDANT LIFE CHURCH
BRADFORD, ENGLAND

Kevin Gerald has a great way of giving practical keys on how to build a healthy mind and a healthy life in *Mind Monsters*. He is able to make the profound applicable to every person and is without a doubt one of the best church leaders I know.

—STEVE KELLY
PASTOR OF WAVE CHURCH
VIRGINIA BEACH, VA

Kevin Gerald has written a book that is in his "sweet spot." *Mind Monsters* will be a great read because Kevin is one the best I know at processing thoughts and preventing them from becoming devastating "mind games." You won't be afraid of monsters anymore when you finish this book.

—MARK CROW
PASTOR OF VICTORY CHURCH
OKLAHOMA CITY, OK

When you read someone's book, you become the beneficiary of his life experience, and that wisdom has the potential to bring about transformation in your own life. Kevin Gerald's book *Mind Monsters* will do just that! *Mind Monsters* is not just a revelation about "invaders of your mind." More importantly, it is about what you can do to stop them! Remember, "When you elevate your thinking, you elevate your life!" Kevin Gerald's book will help you do just that!

—KEITH CRAFT

FOUNDING PASTOR OF ELEVATE LIFE CHURCH AND AUTHOR OF *LEADERSHIPOLOGY 101*

Pastor Kevin offers a useful tool to identify and become more aware of negative thought patterns that hinder growth to turning one's life around after hitting rock bottom. A helpful and practical guide based on truth found in biblical scripture and the promises of Jesus Christ.

—MARION JONES-THOMPSON

AUTHOR OF *ON THE RIGHT TRACK*

Mind Monsters is the perfect title to a book that will show you how to kick out negativity and transform your life. So many struggle in this area and don't realize how quickly and effectively they can have freedom and a mind that works to its optimum. Kevin Gerald is a great communicator. He has an ability to go deep into a issue, making it relevant and easy for anyone to understand and overcome. Each chapter will equip you with skills to get rid of mind monsters and go to a whole new level in life.

—LEON FONTAINE

SENIOR PASTOR OF SPRINGS CHURCH AND CEO OF MIRACLE CHANNEL

Kevin Gerald's book *Mind Monsters* provides tangible and practical weapons to ward off anything false residing in your mind that needs to move out of town. I have always appreciated Kevin's gift to take biblical truth and apply it to our everyday battles in life. Applying the content within this book will gear you up for the battle we all face, the battle within our own minds.

—DINO RIZZO

LEAD PASTOR OF HEALING PLACE CHURCH

KEVIN GERALD

CHARISMA
HOUSE

Most CHARISMA HOUSE BOOK GROUP products are available at special quantity discounts for bulk purchase for sales promotions, premiums, fund-raising, and educational needs. For details, write Charisma House Book Group, 600 Rinehart Road, Lake Mary, Florida 32746, or telephone (407) 333-0600.

MIND MONSTERS by Kevin Gerald
Published by Charisma House
Charisma Media/Charisma House Book Group
600 Rinehart Road, Lake Mary, Florida 32746
www.charismahouse.com

Scripture quotations marked THE MESSAGE are from *The Message: The Bible in Contemporary English*, copyright © 1993, 1994, 1995, 1996, 2000, 2001, 2002. Used by permission of NavPress Publishing Group.

Cover design by Justin Evans
Design Director: Bill Johnson

Visit the author's website at www.kevingerald.tv.

Library of Congress Cataloging-in-Publication Data:

Gerald, Kevin.
Mind monsters / Kevin Gerald. -- First edition.
pages cm
Includes bibliographical references.
ISBN 978-1-61638-738-9 (trade paper) -- ISBN 978-1-61638-739-6 (e-book)
1. Anxiety--Religious aspects--Christianity. 2. Depression, Mental--Religious aspects--Christianity. 3. Healing--Religious aspects--Christianity. 4. Christian life. I. Title.
BV4908.5.G48 2012
248.4--dc23

                    2011048113

First Edition

12 13 14 15 16 — 9 8 7 6 5 4 3 2 1
Printed in the United States of America

DEDICATION

To MY DAUGHTER, Jodi, who completed a fantastic career as a student athlete at Western Washington University in the spring of 2005.

Jodi, when you stepped out of your "safe world" and into the high-pressure world of collegiate athletics, none of us knew the mind monsters that awaited you. Armed with your faith and determination, you excelled as a student while earning your bachelor's degree in business, and you became a team leader and star athlete on the basketball court. You stayed true to your dreams and were a great example of a true Christian in a liberal, secular environment.

Only your mom and I know the many mind monsters you defeated along the way. You're a champion!

CONTENTS

INTRODUCTION

YOU'VE PROBABLY NEVER heard of Roger Babson, even though he is a picture of success in the modern era. This brilliant mathematician and businessman became a millionaire when he formed a financial analysis company just a few years after graduating from the Massachusetts Institute of Technology (MIT). He became a sought-after columnist for popular magazines and newspapers, and he even foresaw the stock market crash of 1929 using an economic assessment technique he developed.

But Babson's main obsession was gravity. When Babson was a child, his sister drowned in a swimming accident, and he believed gravity was to blame. He called it "a dragon" that "came up and seized her."[1]

Decades later Babson's grandson also died tragically by drowning, and this incident seemingly led Babson to found the Gravity Research Foundation as a means of discovering scientific advancements to help mankind conquer the deadly force of gravity. The man went all out in trying to defeat a force he called "Our Enemy Number One."[2]

Now it would seem to me that you don't graduate from a high-profile university like MIT and then enjoy a successful career as a businessman by disconnecting yourself from reason. And yet here was a man, Roger Babson, who was just like the rest of us in many ways—except in his obsession to defeat one of the fundamental forces in our universe. What drove him to have such a disregard for reality, at least in this area?

Hurt. Pain. Heartache from the past. Instead of accepting that life brings both good and bad, Roger Babson allowed thoughts into his mind that drove him to some outlandish pursuits.[3]

So what about you? Do you have some Roger Babson–like thoughts occasionally? Did a painful divorce cause you to say, "I'll never open my heart like that again"? Or did a business failure make you think, "I don't have what it takes to be a success"? Or maybe you feel satisfied in life yet face challenges in your thoughts, moods, and emotions sometimes. Take a minute to think about these questions:

- Do you find yourself focusing on the troubles around you?

- Do you lack peace? Are you conflicted?

- Do you have trouble seeing the good things in your life?

- Do you feel despair or depression, despite the apparent blessings around you?

- Do you go so far as to blame gravity—or some other force—for the hurt and pain in your life?

If you answered yes to one or most of those questions, you may be experiencing mind monsters. Mind monsters are those negative thoughts we all battle, the creeping shadows in the corners of our minds that feed our insecurities, worries, and fears; the thoughts that lead us to irrational anger or undefined depression.

But I have good news for you: with God's help, mind monsters can be defeated! It's not just up to you or me to get rid of mind monsters. God wants us to partner with Him to overcome the negative invaders of our minds. That means He is asking you to take an active role in recognizing, rejecting, and replacing mind monsters you may be facing, as well as in retraining your mind to keep them from returning. We'll spend some time on these four Rs in upcoming chapters. They have helped me tremendously in my own life to partner with God and overcome negative thinking.

We are encouraged, as Christ-followers, to recognize and destroy thoughts that are inconsistent with God's thoughts: "We demolish arguments and every pretension that sets itself up against the knowledge of God, and we take captive every thought to make it obedient to Christ."[4] One of the most potent ways we can take every thought captive and get rid of mind monsters is to build up our faith and fill our mind with the right things.

My goal in writing this book is to equip you to do just that—to learn how to take your thoughts captive and focus only on the ones you *want* to focus on. Let's recognize mind monsters for what they are and learn biblical truths to overcome them. You do not have to spend the rest of your life attached to the mind monsters that may be plaguing you right now. You can discover them, destroy them, and live the best possible life God has for you!

CHAPTER 1

NEGATIVE INVADERS
OF THE MIND

HAVE YOU EVER had the wrong thing in mind? Have you ever had one of those moments when it dawned on you, "I haven't been thinking right"? It's as if a light suddenly comes on, and you realize you've been giving a voice to mind monsters, those negative invaders that come and:

- Steal your joy and peace

- Disrupt your relationships

- Take away your contentment in life

They steal your life, one day at a time. As you read this book, you may be thinking, "I attend church. I've given my life to Christ. I shouldn't have to deal with mind monsters, right?" The truth is, a person can be saved and on his way to heaven and *still* have to battle mind monsters.

So if you want your life experience to be positive, abundant, joyful, and overflowing with peace; if you want to live a successful Christian life with a great marriage and a fantastic relationship with your kids, you have to take a stand against negative invaders of the mind. It's impossible to live a positive life with a negative mind.

Mind monsters are nothing new. In fact they are at least as old as the Bible, all the way back to the Book of Judges, where we can read about a man named Gideon who had to conquer some mind monsters on his way to defeating the Midianites.

The Israelites were in trouble. Their land had been taken over by the Midianites, and they were feeling the weight of oppression. In the middle of this was a lowly farmhand named Gideon. In Judges 6:14, God appears to Gideon and tells him, "Go in the strength you have and save Israel out of Midian's hand. Am I not sending you?"

Pretty strong words to hear directly from God Himself. And yet Gideon immediately let a mind monster jump between him and God. In the very next verse, he replies, "Pardon me, my Lord, but how can I save Israel? My clan is weakest in Manasseh, and I am the least in my family" (v. 15). Can you believe it? *God* just gave Gideon a job, and Gideon refuses, saying he isn't strong enough.

Fortunately when God chooses you, you stay chosen. Gideon essentially spends the rest of the chapter disbelieving God, and God spends the rest of the chapter convincing Gideon that he is, in fact, the one chosen to rescue Israel from their captivity. And from then on, Gideon finally accepts his role and kicks the invaders out. (It's a great story—read Judges 6–8 for all of it.)

There's also the New Testament story of Joseph, where a

mind monster almost kept him from marrying the mother of Jesus. When we read the story of Jesus's birth, it's easy to see how close Joseph came to messing up God's plan. The Bible records in the first chapter of Matthew that Mary and Joseph were engaged to be married. Back in those days if you were engaged, you were committed; it took a divorce to become unengaged.

But then the unthinkable happened, which we read about in Matthew 1:18: "Before [Joseph and Mary] came together, she was found to be pregnant [through the power] of the Holy Spirit" (AMP). When Joseph found out Mary was pregnant, he knew it wasn't *his* child. He also knew Mary's penalty could be death—it was a horrible disgrace for a woman to be pregnant out of wedlock. His decision? *"He had in mind to divorce her quietly."*[1]

He had in mind! Notice how his thinking had gone off course. His mind was on a completely different track than the plan of God. An angel came along and pointed this out to Joseph. I imagine the conversation went something like this: "Joseph, you've got the wrong thing in mind. God's got a plan going on here, and you're not thinking right. You've got to get the right thing in your mind."[2]

If you want to live a successful Christian life, you have to take a stand against the negative invaders of your mind.

WAYWARD THINKING

Have you ever felt sad the moment you woke up? Your mind is whining, "Oh boy, another day! Oh my, a blue Monday! A

3

terrible Tuesday! A weird Wednesday! A tough Thursday! A frightening Friday! A stinking Saturday!"

These wayward thoughts cause you to turn on your country western music and sing, "It's raining outside, and it's raining inside too. I've got trouble on my mind, and I don't know what to do."

What happened to "This is the day the LORD has made; [I will] rejoice and be glad in it"?[3] It went out when sadness came in. The sadness created wayward thoughts, and the mind monster of sadness started jumping around inside your mind wreaking havoc! It said, "Let's go claim Monday as a day of sadness. Let's go ahead and move into Tuesday and call it terrible."

When the mind monster is at work, everything is sad, everything's gloomy—but there's really no reason for it to be that way. The negative invader of your mind came in and created wayward thoughts—thoughts that would get you off course. God had an assignment for you that day. You were supposed to go to work happy. You were supposed to walk in and smile at the folks in the office, greeting them with good cheer.

You were supposed to let your light shine before men so they could see your good works and then honor and glorify God.[4] That was God's plan before sadness—the monster—invaded your mind. Now you're on a completely different track, feeling bad and walking into the office with your head hanging low. When your coworker asks, "Did you have a good weekend?" you can barely respond. You're moping around and sacrificing influence with your poor attitude.

4

You've just been taken over by a mind monster. Get back on assignment and live out the purpose God has for you by understanding that these wayward thoughts are really mind monsters trying to hijack your day and your destiny.

THE TRAINS OF THOUGHTS

A few years ago my wife and I celebrated our wedding anniversary with a trip to Europe. Most of the time we were away we were transported between cities and countries by train. It was an experience that turned out to be much more difficult than we imagined. The signage was insufficient, and finding someone to help us with directions seemed impossible. We ended up being confused for a good portion of the trip. It wasn't until the end of our time in Europe that we began to understand the routing system and train-car assignments.

Have you ever taken a train? If so you know you don't get on one without knowing where it's going. After all that's the whole point; you're on board to get somewhere. In my book *Forces That Form Your Future*, I wrote about the way thoughts are like trains—they take you somewhere. But so often we jump on these trains of thought without knowing our destination!

So many people end up in places they don't want to be and then wonder how they got there. But it only makes sense that they boarded a train of thought to Self-Pity City, Anger Town, or Lonesomeville without even realizing it.

Many times they assume God put them there. I've heard people say, "You know, God put me in this wilderness. I'm hungry, and I can't feed my kids, but God put me here." That usually is not the case. More often than not, God is saying, "I didn't put you there. You boarded the wrong train of thought." The wrong train carries:

- Thoughts of worry

- Thoughts that create guilt

- Thoughts that cause you to feel insecure and question yourself

- Thoughts that bring sadness

- Thoughts that cause suspicion of others' motives

- Thoughts that bring doubt of God and His Word

- Thoughts of inaccurate assumptions

For example, have you ever met a person who assumed something about you that wasn't true? I remember a day when I left church quickly to catch a plane for a speaking engagement. My assistant had picked up a sandwich from Subway for me because I didn't have time to eat lunch. I raced to the airport with no time to spare.

When I arrived, I jumped out of the car, hurried to the check-in counter, and said, "Is there any way you can get me on the plane? Can you get my baggage checked through? I have a speaking engagement tonight, and I've got to get on this plane."

I remember watching the attendant work slowly. I was

wondering, "What's bothering him? Why is he treating me this way?"

Finally he blurted out, "The next time you're running late to the airport, don't take the time to stop at Subway and pick up a sandwich."

Now in that moment I didn't have to be a great man of God to recognize the mind monster of anger that jumped into my thoughts. Longing to leap over the counter and grab the attendant by the neck, I saw a flash, a picture of that negative imagination.

I rebuked that thought. I cast it down. I brought my thoughts into captivity and kindly responded with something like, "I really didn't get the sandwich myself, but that's OK. Would you just please let me on the airplane?"

Thoughts are like trains—
they take you somewhere.

Everyone makes inaccurate assumptions from time to time. The man at the ticket counter put two and two together and assumed I stopped and hung out at Subway and as a result was late for my flight.

He concluded that he shouldn't have had to rush. He probably told himself, "This tardy customer isn't going to create an emergency for me! I've been here all day waiting for him to get here. He obviously stopped at Subway, and now he wants to fire me up and get me going. I'm not hurrying for him, because I know what happened. I see the bag in his hand!"

I have to admit, I'm not immune to making inaccurate assumptions myself. As a Pentecostal preacher's kid, I grew up assuming certain things about people who weren't part of our specific brand of Christianity. It seemed to me that those in other denominations were less informed, less sincere, and just all-around less spiritual than those of us in my dad's church. I stereotyped them as not being on "our side."

But then along came Reggie. We met during football camp while we were in high school and hit it off right away. We saw eye-to-eye on a lot of things and had many of the same interests, including several classes together. He was a fun, good-natured guy and a terrific athlete, so we became friends.

Then I discovered the worst: he was not only one of "them"— his dad was the pastor of one of those *"other"* churches! Yet here we were: two preachers' kids in a large, secular high school. I began to realize that our commonalities were so great they rendered our differences irrelevant, and I stopped making all those negative, incorrect assumptions.

Looking back I can see that God had a bigger plan for me and that even then He was beginning to free me from false assumptions. He was preparing me for what I enjoy now: friendships and camaraderie with pastors and leaders of various doctrinal and denominational backgrounds. My world is so much bigger today than it ever could have been had I held on to my "us and them" mentality. I had to change my mind to change my world.

Every day you're going to be bombarded with mind monsters coming to steal your joy, take away your confidence, mess up your relationships, tempt you to doubt God's Word, keep you focused on your flaws and shortcomings, and create chaos and havoc. There's no condemnation in the fact that mind monsters are lurking in your life—everyone has them. But you have a choice: Will you allow them to stay, affecting who you are and God's plan for your life, or will you conquer them?

KEYS TO REMEMBER

- Mind monsters are the negative invaders of your mind that come to steal your joy and peace, disrupt your relationships, and take away your contentment in life.

- It's impossible to live a positive life with a negative mind.

- If you want to live a successful Christian life, you have to take a stand against the negative invaders of your mind.

- You can overcome the invasion of mind monsters and live according to the assignment God has for you each day.

- Thoughts are like trains; they take you somewhere.

- You have a choice of whether or not you will allow mind monsters to stay, affecting who you are and God's plan for your life, or if you will conquer them.

THINK ABOUT IT

- What do you think about the statement made in this chapter, "I've given my life to Christ. I shouldn't have to deal with mind monsters, right?" Why do you agree or disagree with that statement?

- What are some ways you have learned to conquer mind monsters by reading this book so far? What kinds of things do you already put into practice that help you overcome mind monsters?

- What are some examples of different trains of thought? What do those trains look like when they "arrive" in your mind? (For example, the "Lonesomeville Train" begins with thoughts such as, "No one cares about me.")

- Can you think of a time when you realized, "I haven't been thinking right"? What did you do when you came to that conclusion? Did you take any steps in that moment to begin thinking better? Will you approach that situation differently in the future?

CHAPTER 2

F.A.I.T.H. IS THE EXTERMINATOR

WHAT DO YOU think of when you read the word *faith*? You may think of all the negative comments you've heard, including claims that people of faith are sadly mistaken, naïve, and uneducated. But the fact is, knowledge, understanding, and wisdom are compatible with a life of faith.

Some people would say faith is just another word for religion. Others might look at faith as a mystical power or belief, like some sort of incantation or spell that magically makes everything better. And then there are those who boil faith down to nothing more than a power-of-positive-thinking message—"If you'll just have faith in the positive, everything will turn out all right."

None of these assumptions are correct. They are misleading labels that have little or nothing to do with a biblical interpretation of faith. We find a simple definition in the Book of Hebrews, which tells us, "The fundamental fact of existence is that this trust in God, this faith, is the firm

11

foundation under everything that makes life worth living. It's our handle on what we can't see."[1]

Faith is a trust in God, a belief that He knows what He's doing, regardless of the external circumstances. I want you to think of faith as the exterminator of mind monsters. People who possess a strong presence of faith automatically have fewer problems with mind monsters than those who don't. They are more likely to succeed in life because they have less interference from the negative invaders of the mind.

MIND MONSTER EXTERMINATIONS FOUND IN THE BIBLE

The Bible is packed with stories of people who relied on their faith in God to overcome and exterminate mind monsters. For starters we have Moses, who was rescued as a baby by the pharaoh's daughter. He was an Israelite who was raised as an Egyptian. Later he had to flee from his Egyptian family and rejoin the Israelites. Now an outsider in his own country Moses settled down to become a shepherd and raise a family. That's when God found him.

You probably know the high points. Moses finds the burning bush, where God tells him he's going to be the one to release the Israelites from their bondage to the Egyptians. But do you know Moses's first reaction? He said, "Who am I, that I should go to Pharaoh and bring the Israelites out of Egypt?"[2]

A mind monster stepped right between Moses and God's plan for his life. Moses's background in the world of Egyptian royalty made him the *perfect* person to go speak to

Pharaoh. Yet Moses questioned God's choice of him. Talk about negativity!

But Moses saw God's hand at work, and with God's reassurances and the help of his brother, Aaron, Moses was able to do exactly what God told him to do, which was to lead the Israelites out of Egypt and put them on the road to the Promised Land.

Want another example? Let's fast-forward almost five hundred years to the time of King Solomon, the son of David, Israel's most popular king. There was a bit of a power struggle when it came time for David to die and pass on the kingship, and he appointed Solomon above his son Adonijah, who was next in line.

A little while later, after Solomon's rule was firmly established, he went to worship God, who then appeared to him and said, "Ask for whatever you want me to give you."[3] Solomon was already waist-deep in kinghood and automatically knew the mind monster he was up against.

He understood he wasn't up to the task of ruling Israel, so he said, "Now, O LORD my God, you have made your servant king in place of my father David. But I am only a little child and do not know how to carry out my duties. Your servant is here among the people you have chosen, a great people, too numerous to count or number. So give your servant a discerning heart to govern your people and to distinguish between right and wrong. For who is able to govern this great people of yours?"[4]

Solomon asked God for wisdom, and God's response was truly amazing. He gave Solomon wisdom, yes, but He also gave him wealth and honor to go along with it. And because of these gifts, Solomon became a wise ruler, a prolific writer (most of Proverbs is attributed to him, as well as Ecclesiastes and Song of Solomon), a skilled negotiator, and the architect of the first temple of God. Not too bad. And it was all because he had faith in God's abilities over his own.

One more example, this time from the New Testament, where we meet a guy named Saul. Talk about dealing with mind monsters. Saul was a hard-line Jew who was doing his best to arrest or kill as many Christians as he could. And then one day he met Jesus in a blinding flash while walking down the road.

The light was so bright it knocked him to the ground, and then came a voice that said, "Saul, Saul, why do you persecute me?"

Saul recognized the voice as being holy in nature, so he replied, "Who are you, Lord?" Everything he thought he knew about faith was being flipped upside down!

"I am Jesus, whom you are persecuting," came the reply.[5]

Put yourself in Saul's shoes. You think you've been doing the right thing, then suddenly, in a literal flash, you discover that not only have you been doing the wrong thing, but you've also been actively working *against* the right one! What sort of mind monsters do you think leaped into action in Saul's brain just then? Probably doubt, insecurity, and pride, just to name a few.

And to make matters worse, he was now blind and had to be led by hand into the city, where he waited for three days for the next word from Jesus. It came through a Christian named Ananias, who, at the request of Jesus, went to Saul and prayed for him. And God immediately restored his sight. From that moment on, Saul lived a dynamic life of faith, eventually changing his name to Paul and writing two-thirds of the New Testament.

This guy had some serious faith in Jesus because he endured *a lot* to preach the message of the gospel. Beatings, incarceration, shipwrecks, nights without food—you name it, he did it. (See 2 Corinthians 11:24–30 for a long list.) But he was able to carry on because of his great faith in God's ability to see him through and to exterminate whatever mind monsters reared their ugly heads.

MODERN FAITH EXTERMINATIONS IN ACTION

When it comes to talking about faith-exterminating mind monsters, it's hard to find an example better than George Müller. Here was a man who was so certain of God's call on his life that he never allowed mind monsters to overcome his faith.

In the mid-1800s, Müller and his wife established five orphanages that eventually cared for more than ten thousand children, and he never once asked anyone for money—nor did he go into debt! Müller simply had faith that God would provide and saw, time and again, God do just that.

One particularly amazing story goes like this: running an orphanage was an expensive proposition, so the Müllers welcomed any and all donations from the surrounding community but never solicited them. One morning the cupboards were completely bare, but the Müllers and the children all sat down at the table for breakfast anyway, confident that God would come through and meet their needs. They prayed and gave thanks for breakfast—the one they didn't even have.

And as soon as Müller said, "Amen," there was a knock at the door. Who should be there but a baker, bringing a donation of fresh bread that was the right amount to feed everyone.[6]

In my own life I've seen God's provision show up just in time with last-minute knocks at the door bringing the answer to our prayer. Did I have some mind monsters leading up to that knock? Sure. Who wouldn't? But God shows up when we stand in faith and stare down mind monsters.

In 1986 I became the pastor of a church that had a mountain of debt, a seemingly insurmountable list of bills that had accumulated before we arrived. The church wasn't very big, and I didn't know what else to do but ask that small group of people to bring their best, one-time offering. Our small church came together, and people gave the best they could, and we raised a grand total of $7,500 on one Sunday. It was small beginnings, but it was our best and we celebrated.

In that moment, however, our annual Liberty Offering was born. None of us could have known it at the time, but that first offering was the beginning of a turnaround for our entire church, the beginning of an amazing journey and a legacy of generous giving.

As we release this book, we have brought in more than $7 million through our annual Liberty Offerings over the last twenty-five years! This offering has helped our ministry move forward by maintaining God's house in many ways, such as building ministry facilities for our children and youth, paying for chairs, paving parking lots, updating technology to communicate the message better, and so much more.

The reality is God's house is more than just a facility that is built or maintained—people's lives are being changed in those buildings. Homes are being healed, and passion for life is being renewed in His house. We're also able to give more to missions and disaster recovery, and to support outreach initiatives both locally and globally through the additional generosity that is displayed in the Liberty Offering each year.

> *When your faith becomes big,*
> *mind monsters become small.*

Faith defeats mind monsters every time! Medical research confirms that those who attend church and behave consistently with their faith are less likely to abuse alcohol or drugs or receive treatment for stress or depression. They are more likely to experience stable relationships and satisfaction in marriage and live healthier, more fulfilling lives.[7]

When your faith becomes big, mind monsters become small. It's impossible to continue to be controlled by negativity when you have a growing presence of faith in your life! This realization anchors you in the understanding of something George Müller understood very well: that faith is the exterminator of mind monsters!

HOW TO BUILD YOUR F.A.I.T.H.

An acronym for faith that has helped me increase its presence and power in my life is:

F—focus on the positive
A—affirm yourself
I—imagine God doing something good in your
   situation
T—trust God in all things
H—hope for the best

This F.A.I.T.H. conquers mind monsters. Let's take a closer look at each of the phrases that make up the F.A.I.T.H. acronym.

FOCUS ON THE POSITIVE

Before he went into ministry, one of my pastor-friends, Leon Fontaine of Springs Church in Canada, trained to be a javelin thrower in the Olympics. Now you don't get to train at an Olympic level if you aren't a pretty good athlete to begin with. Leon was already a good javelin thrower, but he needed to take his skills to the next level.

As he worked with his coaches and trainers day after day, he kept hearing what he was doing wrong. This put his focus on trying to correct himself, but the more he focused on what was wrong, the worse his performance became.

Then one of his coaches gave him a video of the world's best javelin thrower. Instead of focusing on his own shortcomings and flaws, Leon studied the champion's form and focused on the way he did things. Over and over he watched the way he released the javelin; Leon examined the best of the best and incorporated those techniques into his own style.

Instead of focusing on the negative, creating a "don't do

this" mentality, he switched it up to a "do it like this" mind-set. Unsurprisingly, when he changed his focus, Leon's performance improved immediately!

Similarly on any given day we all possess good and bad in our lives. As you're reading this book, you're bearing your share of troubles and enjoying your share of blessings in life. Your faith will grow when you focus on the positive!

Every day you must decide what you're going to focus on. God won't decide for you—*you* must decide what your focus will be. Ask yourself this question: "Has my life improved when I've focused on all the negative things around me?" Positive minds produce positive lives; negative minds produce negative lives. Positive minds are always full of faith; negative minds are always full of mind monsters.

AFFIRM YOURSELF

What do you say to yourself all day long? Don't underestimate the effect your internal dialogue has on your faith. (Internal dialogue is what you say to yourself. We'll talk more about it in chapter 3.)

Are you allowing monsters of self-doubt to lead you down paths of insecurity and low self-worth? Instead why not identify with the "you" who is in the metamorphosis of God's plan—the "you" God is creating rather than the "you" of your past or the "you" of your present!

Right now maybe you're a caterpillar, but thank God you're on your way to becoming a butterfly. You can either think of the "you" who is struggling to break out—the weak, little, wingless caterpillar. Or you can focus on the "you" who is free, with wings strong enough for you to fly around and function the way God created you to.

If you've ever experienced the joy of building a house, you know how much fun it is to drive out to the property when it's just a pile of dirt and the foundation is being poured. You invite your friends, and they all come along just to be nice. With blueprints in hand, you tell them, "The kitchen's going to be here, and the bedroom is going to be there. It's going to be this color. And the garage isn't going to be a one-car garage but a three-car garage."

And your friends say, "That's beautiful. That's awesome. Now can we go and get something to eat?" But it doesn't faze you that your friends are not wowed by what they see, because while the house is under construction, you're excited about what will be, not what is.

Your enemy, the mind monster, wants you to focus on what you see in your life right now: all of your failures and shortcomings, the "you" who doesn't measure up. He wants you to focus on the dirt and mud and the ugly concrete foundation. That's what he wants you to think of as "you." But God is saying, "No, there's a champion inside of you!"

You may not feel like it yet, but you are on your way to being exactly what God wants you to be. As Paul says in Philippians 1:4–6, "I always pray with joy because of your partnership in the gospel from the first day until now, being confident of this, that he who began a good work in you will carry it on to completion until the day of Christ Jesus." Don't get caught up in just what exists today. Speak positive things to yourself! Speak life into your future! You are a work in progress, and God isn't finished!

Repentance as a means of affirming yourself

While you don't want to focus only on your weaknesses, it is good to recognize things that hold you back so you can acknowledge when you've messed up and repent. The word *repentance* literally means "turning from your old ways." When you repent, you completely turn away from the sin and face out toward the new you. Repentance is not just feeling sorrow for your sin; it's a courageous move in an entirely new direction.

Some people never get up from the "sackcloth and ashes" mode of repentance to start moving on with their lives. Instead mind monsters of shame use guilt and condemnation to hold them captive. This is why it's so important not only to have an awareness of your sin but also to have an awareness of God's extravagant love for you and His outrageous grace that is always, constantly extended toward you.

I'm sure if I had not received this revelation of God's love and grace I would have given up being a pastor a long time ago. I'm so far from perfect. I'm impatient. I have bad days when my attitude is wrong and I can't seem to get it right. I can be unfair. I can be biased. Sometimes I don't live up to my own standard of righteous living. Sometimes I even get discouraged and question God.

So what can I do? I can throw my hands up and take on the shame of my own failures. Or I can put my faith in Christ, repent, and receive an abundance of grace and the gift of righteousness. Romans 5:17 tells us that "those who receive God's abundant provision of grace and of the gift of righteousness reign in life." I can reign! You can reign! While you're working out repentance in your life—your habits, your strengths, and your weaknesses—don't leave the position God has given you as a grace-receiving child of His who is in right standing with Him.

Instead hold your position with confidence and watch your defeats lessen and your victories increase. At first you may be inconsistent while trying to live a life victorious over sin. You may start off going from defeat to defeat. But then you'll see yourself going from defeat to defeat to victory to defeat. As you get stronger, you'll start to see yourself going from defeat to victory to defeat to victory. You see what I'm saying? Finally you'll find yourself going from victory to victory to victory!

The important thing is to continue affirming yourself throughout this whole process. Affirm your *true* identity as a man or woman of God so you don't give up in the face of your own failures.

Repentance in action: King David

We see repentance in action in the Book of 2 Samuel, when King David got so twisted by lust that he committed adultery with Bathsheba, got her pregnant, then had her husband murdered so he could marry her in hopes of covering up his sinful indiscretion.

You know what led to David's adulterous act in the first place? David was at home when he shouldn't have been: "In the spring, at the time when kings go off to war, David sent Joab out with the king's men and the whole Israelite army."[8]

Instead of going off to war, David was home alone, and we have to wonder if he didn't have sin on his mind in the first place.

So David spies Bathsheba one night, sends for her, takes her to bed; then the lies and murder come into the picture. He thought he'd gotten away with committing adultery and murder, but we see that, though he may have fooled everyone else, he couldn't fool God. We read in 2 Samuel 11:27 that "the thing David had done displeased the LORD."

God used the prophet Nathan to confront David, who finally came clean and admitted his wrongdoing. God forgave his sin, but as one of the consequences of his actions, David lost the son who had been conceived in adultery.

Then look at what happened next. We read in 2 Samuel 12:29: "David mustered the entire army and went to Rabbah, and attacked and captured it." David repented. He turned away from his sinful ways and got back to doing what he was supposed to be doing in the first place—going out with his army and doing the work of *being the king*. And God gave him and his army the victory.

It's worth noting that David didn't stay depressed about the terrible tragedy he brought upon his family. He knew he had made a giant mistake, and that mistake had ricocheted all the way into his family line. He picked up the pieces and moved forward, apologetic and wiser.

This is the key to repentance: changing your ways, moving on, and affirming yourself. When you repent, you must remind yourself that you have the mind of Christ[9] instead of chastising yourself for making another mistake. Say, "I can do all things through Christ who strengthens me"[10] when you feel you don't measure up. Don't give up! Affirm yourself!

IMAGINE GOD DOING SOMETHING GOOD IN YOUR SITUATION

OK, let's get back to our F.A.I.T.H. acronym. "F" is focus on the positive, and "A" is affirm yourself. Now "I" is imagine God doing something good. I thank God for the power of imagination! He gave it to you and me to use for our good.

Therefore when you pray, imagine your problem disappearing. When you pray, imagine your prayer being answered. Imagine your prodigal son or daughter, brother or sister, mom or dad coming to Christ or recommitting his or her life to Him. Imagine a job headed your way that you've been praying about and believing God for. Imagine yourself being open to doing anything for Him—whatever He puts in your hands. Imagine God at work doing something good for you!

You can imagine this because the Bible tells us God *wants* good things for us. We need look no further than Jeremiah 29:11, where God says, "I know the plans I have for you...plans to prosper you and not to harm you, plans to give you a hope and a future." We also have a wonderful hope expressed in Isaiah 55:8–9: "For my thoughts are not your thoughts, neither are your ways my ways....As the heavens are higher than the earth, so are my ways higher than your ways and my thoughts than your thoughts." We all need some of that God-breathed imagination! He then goes on to say, "My word that goes out from my mouth...will not return to me empty, but will accomplish what I desire and achieve the purpose for which I sent it."[11]

In August of 2004 my wife, daughter, and I were in an accident in Bermuda. Lying in a hospital room with a broken pelvis, I remember battling my thoughts. I wondered, "Why did this happen to me? Here of all places, where there isn't even a good hospital!"

Eight days passed before the staff cleaned out the deep wounds in my leg. I was wrestling with so many questions: "Why, God? I'm Your son. I'm a man of God. How could this happen to me here?"

The song "My Hope Is in the Name of the Lord" inspired new hope and expectation within me. While listening to it repeatedly, I began to imagine my health restored. I started telling myself: "I'm going to leave this place. I'm going to be well. I'm going to be healthy. Some great things are going to happen to people I meet here through this situation I'm in."

I thank the Lord that great things did happen while I was there. I thank God for healing me. I'm whole, and I'm well. I've gotten better and stronger every day. Someone asked me, "Pastor, if you could go back in time and avoid that accident in your life, would you?" Honestly, from my heart, I can't say I wish this event never occurred because of all the good things that have happened as a result.

I really believe all the good things were stimulated to happen because in my mind's eye I saw God at work. I imagined how God was moving in that specific situation in my life right then. I still imagine Him at work in my life now.

Do you realize that right at this moment, God is working

invisibly in your life to bring good things to you? *God is at work!* Imagine Him at work.

TRUST GOD IN ALL THINGS

Think of God as always being with you. He's present even when you don't see Him. I live in Seattle, and if you don't know this about the Pacific Northwest, it's often overcast here. We don't get a lot of torrential downpours; we have a lot of drizzle and many, many clouds. I love those frequent times when I board a plane on a cloudy day, take off, then break through the clouds to see the sun shining in all its brightness. It's amazing how something that big and powerful can be hidden by clouds.

When you live in a region of seemingly continuous cloud cover, it's easy to forget the sun even exists. We feel its heat in Seattle, but there are times of the year when we seldom see its light. But even in those times when we've been through a long stretch of overcast days, we remember the sun is still there, still shining, still doing its job.

Whether it is covered by the clouds of the sky or the dark of night, the sun never stops shining. We may not see it, but we know it remains; its power is not dependent on the conditions of the earth. Orbiting out here at 93 million miles away, we can't do a single thing to influence the sun's ability to shine.

In the same way when clouds enter some people's lives, they begin to doubt God's presence and goodwill toward them. But He's still there! The sun hasn't stopped shining. Jesus hasn't fallen off His throne. You may not be able to see

Him as easily as you have in the past, but you haven't changed His character and you haven't influenced His abilities.

Isaiah 26:3 says, "You will keep in perfect peace him whose mind is steadfast, because he trusts in you." And we also have this promise from Jesus, just before He ascended into heaven: "Surely I am with you always, to the very end of the age."[12] You may not feel like Jesus is with you in your distress, but He is. You *can* trust Him.

HOPE FOR THE BEST

Hope is what leads you to faith; you can't have faith without it. "Faith is being sure of what we hope for and certain of what we do not see."[13]

The best way to live your life is from a faith-initiated view of tomorrow. For example, imagine I said I wanted to bless you, so I planned to send you on a very lucrative treasure hunt. Let's say I told you that tomorrow between 6:00 a.m. and 6:00 p.m. I had arranged for $1,000 to be placed in ten different locations waiting for you. I would give you the addresses, but you'd have to make sure you picked them up between 6:00 a.m. and 6:00 p.m.

With hope and expectation in your heart, you would begin immediately to arrange your schedule so you would have gained $10,000 by the end of the day (of course, dropping off your tithe before going home!). You would call work and request the day off. You would set your alarm clock early enough to reach the first pickup point at 6:00 a.m. You might have to find transportation. You might even have to hire someone to take care of your children. But you would gladly do all of this, knowing you would be $10,000 richer at the end of the day!

What if you lived your life this way, expecting great things from a God who wants to bless you and has treasures planned for you? All of your plans, actions, efforts, and attention would be focused on Him, expecting what God has promised to provide. Hope is the expectation of good things. So why not hope for the best?

When you're hoping for the best, you're simply hoping for God's promises to be fulfilled in your life. Hoping for the best means you sow with *the expectation* of reaping. When you're hoping for the best, you're fully convinced that your own acts of generosity and kindness toward others will come back to you. Hoping for the best is believing that if you work hard and do what you can, God will open up doors of opportunity and prosper you.

We hope for the best because it's God's plan to give us whatever we need—not just to survive or barely get by, but to have everything we need to fulfill His plan and purpose for our lives. Paul wrote to the church in Philippi and promised, "My God will meet all your needs."[14] I want to encourage you to define your need with an awareness of God's nature and generosity.

God introduced Himself to His people as "Jehovah-Jireh, the Lord God Our Provider" and as "El Shaddai, the God of More Than Enough." Much later, Jesus said, "I have come that they may have life, and that they may have it more abundantly."[15]

So when it's time for you to believe God to meet all your

needs, think of Him as wanting to meet all the needs you have. Think of Him as wanting to provide a home for you, a place to raise your family; an education; transportation; employment; and enough money for you to give like you want to and retire without having to be a burden on your family.

See God as Someone who will meet all your needs and place your hope in that! His provision may not be on your timetable; it may not come as quickly as you imagined. But that is what hope is all about. Hope is what we do to strengthen and build our faith; it ultimately leads us *to* faith.

Another way to build up your faith is by confessing your hope continually. I was never what I would call unhappy, but I had a "bent" toward being melancholy—too melancholy. When I was a young man, a pastor-friend told me to get up in the morning, look in the mirror, and say to myself, "I am happy, I am healthy, and I'm a Christian."

I remember how uncomfortable I was the first few days I did it. The mind monster kept answering me, "No, you aren't. No, you aren't. *No, you aren't!*" But I kept confessing my faith, and I remember the result. When I visited my sister, whom I hadn't seen in a long time, she said, "Kevin, I've noticed how much happier you seem to be. Your face looks happy."

Confessing "I am happy, I am healthy, and I'm a Christian" caused my faith to grow, which overpowered the melancholy invader of my mind. To overcome mind monsters build your confidence in God until the force of faith inside you is stronger than the pressure of the negative invaders against you.

There's a story in the Bible about a man who built up his faith through a positive daily confession. You may know him as Abraham, but he was originally called Abram, and we read about his confession in Genesis 17:4–6. God says to him: "You will be the father of many nations. No longer will you be called Abram; your name will be Abraham, for I have made you a father of many nations. I will make you very fruitful; I will make nations of you, and kings will come from you."

Perhaps I should back up a bit. At this point in his life, Abraham was a well-to-do man who loved his wife but had no natural-born son as an heir. He was getting up in years and had resigned himself just to dying without an expansive family line to carry on his legacy.

And then here comes God, telling him that he was going to be the "father of many nations" and changing his name! But you know what? When God changed his name, He changed his confession. *Abram* means "exalted father," which is high and mighty enough, but God changed his name to *Abraham*, which means "father of many."

So every time Abraham said his own name, every time his wife called him, every time he was addressed by any of his servants, his faith was built up. He was being called "father of many," regardless of the circumstances or situations.

That is a powerful confession, and God made good on His promise. About a year later Abraham's son Isaac was born, and God continued blessing Abraham with subsequent generations. In fact the Bible even says that those who have faith are children of Abraham.[16] If you're a Christian, *you're* a part of God's fulfilled promise to Abraham!

TWO LIONS: FAITH AND FEAR

Two lions wage war inside you—faith and fear. Whichever lion you feed will grow. Feed the lion of faith so it will grow, and starve the lion of fear so it will weaken and die. Decide to grow your faith every day of your life. When it grows, you'll have less of a problem overcoming mind monsters in your everyday life.

Purposely grow your faith, and use it to defeat mind monsters. Focus on the positive, affirm yourself, imagine God doing something good in your life, trust God in everything, and hope for the best!

KEYS TO REMEMBER

- Faith is a trust in God, a belief that He knows what He's doing, regardless of the external circumstances.

- Faith is the exterminator of mind monsters. Faith defeats mind monsters every time!

- F.A.I.T.H. = Focus on the positive, Affirm yourself, Imagine God doing something good, Trust God in all things, and Hope for the best.

- Affirm your true identity as a man or woman of God so you don't give up in the face of your own failures.

- To overcome mind monsters build your faith until the force of faith inside you is stronger than the pressure of the negative invaders against you. When your faith becomes big, mind monsters become small.

- Two lions wage war inside you—faith and fear. Whichever lion you feed will grow.

THINK ABOUT IT

- What does F.A.I.T.H. stand for? How does this acronym help you in your understanding of what faith is and can be in your life?

- Has your life improved when you've focused on all the negative things around you? What are some ways you can focus on positive things instead of negative things in your life?

- What are some examples of things you can say to yourself all day that would build yourself up? What are some examples of things you could say to others that would build them up?

- Can you think of a time when God was working behind the scenes on your behalf, but you didn't realize it until after you were past that tough season?

CHAPTER 3

RECOGNIZING MIND
MONSTERS

A WHILE AGO I participated in a golf tournament. Each foursome was given a yellow ball. If the team was able to present its yellow ball at the end of eighteen holes, the group qualified for a prize.

One member of a team would play the yellow ball on each hole, from the moment he teed off until he putted the ball into the cup. Then he would pass the ball to another teammate, who would play the ball on the next hole and so on.

My team's goal was to make sure we still had that yellow ball at the end of eighteen holes! Every time it was someone's turn to play the ball, the other three guys would warn, "Don't mess up! Make sure it doesn't go in the pond. Make sure it doesn't go in the woods. Hit the ball straight. Play it safe. Keep the yellow ball!" We would cheer for one another, challenging the guardian of the yellow ball.

I had a special event to attend that night, so I had to leave after nine holes. Rushing I threw my golf clubs in the car and was heading out toward the highway when my cell phone rang. I heard my teammates on the other end of the phone screaming, "You've got the yellow ball!" I felt my pocket, and sure enough, I had it. I didn't even realize I'd held on to it.

That's the way it is with mind monsters. Most people who have them don't even realize it. Before you can overcome a mind monster, you must recognize its presence in your life.

Do you know it's easier to recognize someone else's mind monsters than your own? You may be reading this book and thinking, "I hope my husband (wife, friend, parent, etc.) will read this. He really needs it! Oh, I wish my boss would get a copy—he could definitely use this."

> *Before you can overcome a mind monster,*
> *you must recognize its presence in your life.*

Have you ever heard someone say, "I'm not negative; I'm a realist," and then notice the shocked looks on the faces of their friends and family members? Or perhaps you know someone who has said, "I'm not worried; I'm just concerned." Perhaps you've said that yourself. We place our own spin on our mindsets to lessen the brunt of what we're really dealing with.

But you are not in charge of recognizing mind monsters in others; you can only take care of yourself. Their business is their business, as we are reminded in Matthew 7:1–5: "Do not judge, or you too will be judged...and with the measure you use, it will be measured to you. Why do you look at the speck of sawdust in your brother's eye and pay no attention to the plank in your own eye? How can you say to your brother, 'Let me take the speck out of your eye,' when all the time there is a plank in your own eye? You hypocrite, first take the plank out of your own eye, and then you will see clearly to remove the speck from your brother's eye."

You have a responsibility to recognize your own mind monsters and completely deal with them before you can start diagnosing them in others. Now if you suspect your friends and loved ones might be dealing with a specific mind monster, find an opportunity to mention it, but don't take it upon yourself to fix them. You have enough to worry about with yourself. At least I know I do.

One of the most difficult tasks you have is to see your current situation for what it is, not what you think it might be. We all have a tendency to view our lives as good or bad, usually based on our mood at the moment. If things are going well in our lives, we can overlook problems in some areas. If things are going poorly, we can amplify small things to look horrific. We must find the proper balance between the two.

The interesting thing about mind monsters is that they sound like your own inner voice of reason. It's easy to miss a mind monster when it walks through the doorway of your mind because it sounds so much like you. Its entrance is subtle.

So how do you recognize mind monsters in your life? There are three easy ways. Pay attention to your:

- Internal dialogue

- Moods

- Conversation

INTERNAL DIALOGUE

I want you to consider the following, and do your best not to let your eyes glaze over: "Buffalo buffalo Buffalo buffalo buffalo buffalo Buffalo buffalo." So what is this? While it looks like the word *buffalo* over and over, spiced up with random capitalization, it is actually a grammatically correct sentence. Let me see if I can help you understand it.

First you have to remember there are multiple meanings to the word *buffalo*. It can mean either the animal or one of several cities in the United States (let's pick three, in New York, Iowa, and Montana), or "to bully." Now let's use some synonyms (we'll use *bison* for the animal, even though that's technically a different creature) and see if the sentence can make sense: "Bison from New York that get bullied by bison from Iowa will in turn become bullies of bison from Montana."

I hope that makes a lot more sense than just the word *buffalo* over and over. The reason that first sentence makes our head spin (just look at it again: "Buffalo buffalo Buffalo buffalo buffalo buffalo Buffalo buffalo.") is because our internal dialogue interprets it as nonsense. Our minds check out and assume either there is no solution or the explanation is so complex we cannot comprehend it.

Ask yourself, "What effect is my internal dialogue having on me? How does the dialogue in my head cause me to feel and behave?"

I hope you understand what I mean when I say "internal dialogue." We all have this internal way of speaking to ourselves, whether it's in complete sentences or not. We use it all the time, like when we consider the merits of a lane change during rush hour traffic, where we want to go for lunch, or what we want to eat when we get there.

Sometimes we're aware of our internal dialogue; sometimes it's involuntary and we're only aware of it after the fact. You hear a loud crash in the other room, and your mind immediately jumps to several conclusions as you leap up to investigate. Your heart begins to race, and along the way you picture a host of scenarios in your mind, usually featuring children, blood, and broken limbs. You arrive, breathless and flustered, only to see that the cat knocked a book off the shelf, and you sigh in relief and tell yourself how silly you were being.

That's internal dialogue, both the lightning-fast negative conclusions and the relieved way you chide yourself on having reached those negative conclusions in the first place. This dialogue can seem minor, but it actually has major influence on the way your life goes.

If you get lost in the woods in don't-feed-the-bears territory and *think* you hear the brush moving around you, you'll break out in a cold sweat, your heart will beat wildly, and your knees will knock together. And your internal dialogue is driving it all!

Here's a way to know whether your internal dialogue is helping or hurting you. Think about how it makes you feel. When the voice in your head is talking, are you becoming stronger or weaker? More confident or more timid? Don't simply listen to the word *buffalo* repeat itself. Take charge of your thoughts and put in your own synonyms to make sense of what you hear. Let me show you how.

Internal dialogue in the Bible

We can find all sorts of discussion on this internal dialogue in the Bible. For example, when Paul the apostle wrote to the young preacher, Timothy, he was appealing to him to acknowledge the power of his inner dialogue when it came to preaching the gospel: "For God did not give us a spirit of timidity, but a spirit of power, of love and of self-discipline."[1]

Paul was saying, "God didn't give you that spirit of timidity. You need to recognize that's not coming from God." Paul was giving Timothy permission to go all-out for Jesus, just as he himself had done.

Another time, when writing to a church in Corinth, Paul said, "Look, God hasn't given us a spirit of confusion. God's not the author of confusion."[2] If you're confused, angry, or discouraged, you have mind monsters. If you're judgmental, distrustful, and worried about people liking you, or if you're always assuming the worst, then guess what? You have mind monsters!

So do you recognize and oppose them? Or do you deny that you have them?

Here are a couple more examples in Scripture showing how internal dialogue affected a person's life. In the Book of Matthew, we read about a woman who had been hemorrhaging for twelve years and who came to Jesus for healing. She had finally had enough. The Bible records that, as she touched Jesus's cloak, "she said to herself, 'If I only touch his cloak, I will be healed.'"[3] When the verse reads, "she said to herself," I believe she was directing her internal dialogue to be positive.

She was able to reach Jesus, and when she touched His garment, Jesus looked down on her, saw her, and said, "Take heart, daughter...your faith has healed you."[4] Twelve years of suffering ended just like that. A lot of people were touching Jesus that day, but when *she* touched Him, her faith (and her internal dialogue) got Jesus's attention.

Contrast this with a servant who had a negative internal dialogue. In Matthew 25:14–30 we read a parable Jesus told about three servants. Their master entrusted them with some money—called "talents" depending on the translation you read. The first servant received five talents, the second received two, and the third received one.

When the master required an accounting of the money, he was pleased to find that the servants to whom he had given five and two talents had doubled his money. He promptly rewarded them both.

The master was displeased to discover, however, that the third servant had buried his one talent in the ground. The servant explained, "I knew that you are a hard man, harvesting where you have not sown and gathering where you have not scattered seed. So I was afraid and went out and hid your [money] in the ground."[5]

What was the master's reaction? Instead of rewarding the servant, the master said, "You should have put my money on deposit with the bankers, so that when I returned I would have received it back with interest. Take the [money] from him and give it to the one who has ten...and throw that worthless servant outside."[6] The master wasted no time in punishing him severely.

Ouch! This servant let his internal dialogue take over the driver's seat of his life, creating a fear inside him that caused him to bury the one talent that could have meant prosperity, increase, and growth in his life. By contrast, the sick woman with the positive internal dialogue received what she hoped for.

If you want to recognize mind monsters, take a good look at how your internal dialogue is affecting you.

MOODS

The second way to recognize mind monsters in your life is to pay attention to your moods. Today are you upbeat or down in the dumps? Your feelings spring from your thoughts, and thoughts originate in the mind.

How healthy is your mind? To know, take a good look at your mood! The Bible refers to your mood as the "spirit" of your mind. Ephesians 4:23 tells you to "be constantly renewed in the spirit of your mind [having a fresh mental and spiritual attitude]" (AMP).

It's a good thing to pay attention to your moods, to be aware of the way you are feeling at any given moment. This actually sounds a lot easier than it is! We tend to operate based on our emotions without really giving much thought to the feelings we are indulging. Are you happy, sad, angry, confused, depressed, joyful, solemn, concerned? The list goes on and on! And it's easy to feel any of these things—often at the same time—without really defining it consciously or realizing why we're feeling that way.

So learn to pay attention to your moods, to your emotional state. Learn to discover why you may be feeling the way you do, and then think about whether you *want* to feel that way or not. You'll find that, more often than not, you can change the way you feel by changing the way you think.

As you read this book, you may be thinking about how much you hate mind monsters and want them out of your life. You're thinking about faith and how to grow it. But even though you're focusing on this, some time today something will probably happen that tempts you to feel upset. You may find yourself in a traffic jam that makes you feel annoyed. Why don't you decide to put on some positive music or inspirational teaching so you can renew your mind instead?

If you want to live a victorious Christian life, you have to constantly renew the mood of your mind. Here are just a few strategies that have helped me renew the mood of my mind. This is by no means a comprehensive list, but I hope it will jump-start a new practice in your own life.

Music. There's just something about music that reaches directly to your soul and influences your mood. It's difficult to be really mellow when you're listening to chaotic, up-tempo music, just as it's difficult to be angry when you listen to something soothing and relaxing. When my mood needs to be renewed, I've found a little praise and worship music can be just the thing. Really I find a lot of songs inspire me, whether they're worship, Christian, or secular (such as Tim McGraw's song "Live Like You Were Dying"). Then there are times when, returning from an out-of-town speaking engagement that my wife, Sheila, wasn't able to attend, I will listen to love songs on my iPod that stir up the love I have for her. Whatever the situation, there is usually a song that can help me adjust my mood.

Speaking God's Word. In addition to being a helpful spiritual discipline, speaking Scripture out loud is also a great way to renew the mood of your mind. By speaking positive verses or the promises of God, you are not only declaring God's Word over your life, but you're also helping to internalize its truth in your very soul. In Appendix A you will find a list of great scriptures to help get you started.

Read the Bible. Locate stories in the Bible about people who have gone through the very same struggles you're encountering. Dealing with anger? Look up the troubles of Peter and see how he handled it. Feel like the world is against you? Find comfort in many of the psalms of David. There is a wealth of riches in the Scriptures.

Affirm yourself. Your tongue is a powerful tool, or, as James puts it: "When we put bits into the mouths of horses to make them obey us, we can turn the whole animal. Or take ships as an example. Although they are so large and are driven by strong winds, they are steered by a very small rudder wherever the pilot wants to go. Likewise the tongue is a small part of the body, but it makes great boasts. Consider what a great forest is set on fire by a small spark."[7] Use your tongue correctly, and it will spark a marvelous change in your mood.

Prayer. What an agent of change prayer can be. Pray over your situation, but don't let your prayer life be all about you.

42

Pray for others, and you'll find yourself more and more renewed. Pray for your family, your friends, your spiritual leaders, your actual leaders. Once you get started, it's hard to stop! We'll talk more about effective ways to pray in chapter 5.

CONVERSATION

The third way to recognize mind monsters in your life is to pay attention to your conversation. Let's take a look at a couple named Brenda and Tony. Brenda is constantly nagging Tony about what he's doing wrong and what she doesn't like about him.

She says things such as, "Why do you wear ties? And silver ones at that? And that hair on your face! What a dork you are! You're useless."

You may be thinking, "Wow! I know what needs to happen. Brenda needs Jesus. After she's born again, this issue will go away." That's how a lot of Christians think. Guess what? Brenda *is* saved. Brenda already has Jesus in her life, and she's on her way to heaven!

Brenda is like many Christians. Even though she is saved, Brenda has a problem with mind monsters. Her mind monster causes her to always focus on the negative. She subconsciously thinks she's called to be the fault-finder in her world. Whether the faults are in her kids, her husband, or her job, she spotlights them as if she'll win a reward.

How can she recognize this mind monster of fault-finding? By noticing her critical conversation. In the same way you don't want to underestimate your internal dialogue, don't underestimate the power of the words that come out of your mouth. Pay attention to the conversations you have with people. Do you constantly stir up drama to talk about? Do most of your conversations veer off in a positive direction or a negative one? Are you stuck in a cycle of fault-finding or finding things to compliment?

A good way to find out if you have mind monsters is to pay attention to your conversations. Jesus said, "Out of the abundance of the heart the mouth speaks."[8] So there's a good chance that what is coming out of your mouth is connected to whatever is going on in your heart and head.

THE POWER OF RECOGNITION

Recognizing mind monsters is the first step to eliminating them, while denying their presence allows them to stay. Over the next three days pay attention to your internal dialogue, moods, and conversation. What's there?

It's time to acknowledge the presence of mind monsters. We won't get anywhere by ignoring the problem. If your house were full of termites, wouldn't you want to know? It wouldn't make much sense to stick your fingers in your ears and just hope they go away. If you do that long enough, you'll soon be looking for a new house, because the one you're in will have collapsed!

Also if you start to feel a cold coming on, do you just close your eyes and hope it passes, or do you start taking vitamin C? Ignoring the symptoms of an illness doesn't help you. Actually the opposite is true—disregard your symptoms and they'll likely get worse than if you'd treated them right away because eventually your body is going to shut down and force you to take care of yourself.

In the same way mind monsters are a real threat and problem that must be dealt with. They won't go away on their own, and if you pay no attention to them, they'll likely just get worse.

So think about your internal dialogue, moods, and conversation over the next three days and see what you find. Chances are you will recognize negativity you had somehow overlooked. When you've learned to recognize mind monsters, you'll be ready to move on to the next step and get busy rejecting the influence of mind monsters in your life.

KEYS TO REMEMBER

- Before you can overcome a mind monster, you must recognize its presence in your life.

- Mind monsters often sound like your own inner voice of reason.

- You have a way of speaking to yourself that has a major influence on the way your life goes.

- Feelings originate from thoughts, and thoughts originate in the mind. You can change the way you feel by changing the way you think.

- Renew your mind by listening to music, speaking God's Word, reading the Bible, affirming yourself, and praying.

- Recognize mind monsters in your life by paying attention to your conversation.

- Recognizing mind monsters is the first step to eliminating them, while denying their presence allows them to stay.

THINK ABOUT IT

- The Bible tells us to be constantly renewed in the attitude of our mind.[9] What are some ways to renew the attitude of your mind?

- How can you begin to recognize mind monsters in your life? Do you recognize and oppose them? Or do you deny that you have them? Can you identify two or three that are trying to take root in your life right now?

- Consider what your inner voice has been saying to you. What effect does your internal dialogue have on you? In other words, how does the dialogue in your head cause you to feel and behave? (For example, when the voice in your head is talking, are you becoming stronger or weaker? More confident or more timid?)

- Think back over the last three days. Can you recall your dominant internal dialogue, moods, and conversation? Were they positive or negative? Over the next three days, pay attention to your internal dialogue, moods, and conversation. Challenge yourself to identify what's there.

CHAPTER 4

REJECTING MIND MONSTERS

DO YOU REALIZE that your mind has power to influence and, in some cases, create your reality? Your life will be defined by the thoughts you accept or reject. One day I listened as a neighbor described how he was raising his nine-year-old daughter. He said, "We're not attending one church. We're taking her to all the different places of worship to expose her to a broad spectrum of religions. Then if she doesn't want to go to church, that will be fine. She won't have to go. We're just going to give her a broad, open-minded perspective of everything."

I replied, "So what happens if she doesn't want to go to school tomorrow?"

He exclaimed, "Oh, no! She must go to school because she has to get an education."

So I countered, "Is that an absolute? You're not going to be open-minded about that?"

He said, "No, because education really affects where you go in life."

We live in a time when people are so open-minded they have no "true north" in their lives. They hear a thought and open their mind to it. Then they hear another idea and open their mind to that as well.

> *Your life will be defined by the thoughts you accept or reject.*

They are so open-minded, they end up entertaining every thought that shows up. They have "the inquiring mind." They think, "I want to go investigate that; I want to experience that kind of movie; I want to read that book; I want to listen to that idea; I want to consider that concept."

Eventually they lack discretion and judgment. They adhere to *no* absolutes—they argue with the compass.

TRUE NORTH PRINCIPLES THAT CHANGED THE WORLD

I love the story of William Wilberforce, a man who stuck to his true north principles and literally changed the world. One day in 1787, while in prayer, Wilberforce strongly felt an urge from God, which he recorded in his journal: "God Almighty has placed before me two great objects, the Suppression of the Slave Trade and the Reformation of Manners [moral values]."[1]

And so began what would become a determined, twenty-year odyssey as Wilberforce, a member of the British Parliament, doggedly fought against the slave trade. The story is far too long to be told in detail here (for an excellent take on it, I recommend the film *Amazing Grace*), but here is the gist of it. Year after year, bill after bill, setback after setback,

Wilberforce stayed true to what he knew God had spoken to him—even though it cost him relationships, endangered his health, and damaged his public persona.

Wilberforce, along with a select group of friends and compatriots, did everything he could to change the tide of public opinion when it came to slavery. And after twenty years of effort, he was able to see his dream come to fruition in February 1807 when the House of Commons passed his bill by an overwhelming majority. The first battle in the war against slavery had finally been won, and it was all because of a man who refused to let go of his true north principles.

WHY TRUE NORTH PRINCIPLES?

The true north principles at work in the world were established by God, not by society. You will find them in His Word, where Psalm 1 says, "Blessed (happy, fortunate, prosperous, and enviable) is the man...*[whose]* delight and desire are in...(the precepts, the instructions, teachings of God) *[on which]* he habitually meditates (ponders and studies) by day and by night....Everything he does shall prosper...but the way of the ungodly [those living outside God's will] shall perish."[2]

The more you live in harmony with God's principles, the better your life will be. You will experience greater joy, greater peace, and greater success. The more you ignore these true north principles, the greater the challenges you will encounter, the more lost and abandoned you will feel, and the more insecure and unsure of yourself you will become.

Second Corinthians 10:5 teaches that we must recognize

and destroy thoughts that are inconsistent with God's thoughts: "We demolish arguments and every pretension that sets itself up against the knowledge of God, and we take captive every thought to make it obedient to Christ."

Jesus demonstrated this when Peter expressed his disapproval of Jesus's impending suffering and death. He rebuked Peter, saying "Get behind me, Satan!....You do not have in mind the things of God, but [rather] the things of men."[3] He was rejecting the thought Peter spoke that originated in hell.

JOSIAH: A TRUE NORTH KING

Before we dive directly into defining true north principles, I want to give you an example of someone who discovered them and followed them, regardless of the outcome. That person is Josiah, the king of Judah we read about in 2 Kings 22. Shockingly he became king at the tender age of eight, and he basically just let the country run itself, doing whatever his father had done before him, paying lip service to God while simultaneously offering sacrifices to a bunch of false gods.

Josiah let this kind of anything-goes behavior continue for eighteen years—until the momentous occasion when a high priest in the temple of the Lord found "the Book of the Law," the law of Moses, which had been squirreled away somewhere in the temple and scarcely looked at. The high priest took the book to Josiah's secretary, who then read it to Josiah. And when Josiah heard what the book said—(think along the lines of the Ten Commandments)—he was so distressed he tore his clothes.

Here Josiah was, leading a nation into apostasy without even knowing it! But he had been given a book full of true north principles, showing him the way he and the rest of the people of Judah should be living, so he had a decision to make. Would he keep doing what was comfortable and traditional, or would he take the hard steps of following true north principles, come what may?

Being the smart man that he was, Josiah sought out a prophet for wisdom on how he should proceed. I'd love to say that God responded along these lines: "Tell Josiah that everything will be fine. All he needs to do is tear down all the false gods, and I'll bless the nation of Judah with riches and peace."

I would like to tell you that is the way God responded, but it wasn't. He actually said, basically, "Josiah, I'm going to destroy your nation, and there's nothing you can do about it. But since you want to do what's right, I'll wait to do it until after you're dead."[4]

Josiah obeyed and followed the true north principles he discovered, and as a result spared his nation and the people in it from ruin. Who knows how many people had their lives eternally changed as a result of God's delayed punishment? Who knows how many positive changes swept through the people of Judah as they echoed their king in following true north principles? This is why I encourage everyone to follow true north principles, regardless of the outcome. God will see your efforts and respond!

Now let's look at two principles to help you *accept* true north thoughts and *reject* mind monster thoughts in your life:

1. Commit to a P4:8 standard for your thoughts.

2. Activate a border patrol to guard your mind.

THE P4:8 STANDARD

What is the P4:8 standard for your thoughts? P4:8 stands for Philippians 4:8, which says, "Finally brothers, whatever is true, whatever is noble, whatever is right, whatever is pure, whatever is lovely, whatever is admirable—if anything is excellent or praiseworthy—think about such things."

If a thought is true but not noble, don't think about it. If it's not pure, admirable, or lovely, don't dwell on it. When you hear someone say, "Life is hard; it's so tough!" you don't have to accept it—you can reject that thought. This scripture is saying: don't give mental energy to a thought unless it passes the P4:8 standard.

If you own a champion racehorse you think has a chance to win the Kentucky Derby, you're not going to feed that racehorse ketchup and peanut butter. You're going to look for the highest quality oats you can find. You're going to want to know exactly what's going into the horse's body so you'll know it has what it needs to achieve the greatest results. You understand that feeding the horse the right food directly relates to the horse's performance.

Your mind is more valuable than a racehorse! If you want to position yourself for success, you must accept the fact that what you allow into your mind will affect the outcome of your life.

If you use a computer, you're probably familiar with the

"delete" button. When you scan through your daily e-mails, you identify what you're interested in by looking at the subject lines. When you see something you choose not to take time with, you hit the delete button. Do the same with your thoughts. Delete, delete, delete!

You are the thinker of your own thoughts! It's easy to blame others, such as your parents, the media, or Hollywood influencers. But in reality you choose what you're going to allow in. I remember an occasion years ago when a woman came to me about a problem with her husband. She was ready to get rid of him, just turn him in. He didn't measure up.

I said to her, "Would you do me a favor? Would you just simply go home today and try to find ten good things about your husband this week? If you can find ten good things about him and focus on those qualities, I believe your situation will begin to turn around."

Negative or positive, nothing this wife could do would change her husband's behavior, because *he* decides how he will act. That's *his* decision to make. She can't make his choices for him, even if she wanted to; she can only make *her own* choices about *her own* behavior. She had been making the wrong choice. She had been choosing to focus only on the negative aspects of her husband's behavior, to the point where she couldn't even *see* the positives that were there.

So instead of making a negative choice, she made a positive one. She chose to focus on the good things in her husband, no matter how small they were. Maybe it was the way he took out the trash without being asked or the way he screwed the cap back on the toothpaste tube. Who knows what it was—but she did it.

And wouldn't you know it, by changing her focus, she indirectly challenged her husband to change his. Negativity is a mirror, and I can guarantee that much of his negativity was due to seeing negativity from her. Once he began to see positive things from his wife, he could start making better choices. He could rise to her challenge.

I'm happy to say that now, more than ten years later, I still see this couple in church. They are together and doing extremely well. It seems that in every birthday note or Christmas card I receive from this grateful wife she thanks me for challenging her to focus on the positive in her husband.

After you decide to think only the thoughts that pass the P4:8 standard, set up a border patrol for your mind. This is the action you take to enforce the P4:8 standard, the policing of thoughts that try to steal your success in life.

BORDER PATROL

North of Seattle, Washington, there's a patrol that scrutinizes every person before he or she crosses the border between Canada and the United States. Once when my wife, Sheila, and I were traveling, the Border Patrol agents pulled us out of line and into their building. They thoroughly checked us out.

After it was all over, I enjoyed teasing my wife, telling her that *she* was the one who looked suspicious. I told her I wasn't going to bring her with me the next time. We had a lot of fun with it.

Throughout the examination we expressed our thanks to

the Border Patrol because we understood they were there to reject travelers who planned to hurt our nation. We understood the value of the scrutiny. We appreciated the fact that they were there to protect us.

This is not the only time I've had my world opened up to the real dangers to our borders. One of my favorite sports is big-game hunting, and one year a friend of mine and I made plans to hunt mountain lions in Arizona.

I didn't realize until we arrived that we had booked our hunting adventure in some mountains just east of Nogales, Arizona, the same mountains where National Geographic shoots parts of their reality show *Border Wars*. This place is a notorious location for illegal immigrants and drug smugglers to pour into the United States.

In addition to this the area is home to a group of heavily armed thugs—mostly from South America and Vietnam—who attempt to steal from the people smuggling drugs into the country. These thugs have a lot of firepower and seem almost to relish displaying it.

My friend and I spent four long days in that war zone, seeing and hearing firsthand from the people involved in the battle to protect our border. And in the end we were more successful at finding drugs than mountain lions, because we helped the Border Patrol locate eighty pounds of marijuana.

These people are heroes. Some of the people patrolling our borders are ranchers whose families have owned their land for more than one hundred years. They are determined not to be driven off their ranches by smugglers and violent criminals, even in the face of brutal murders. They carry weapons at all times. These people, along with the US Army, are engaged in constant conflict and are at work day and night.

They are tireless, courageous, tenacious, and effective. They are the embodiment of the type of border patrol we need to have on our own minds. Whatever the cost, whatever it takes—we must guard our minds.

An unguarded mind is an unprotected mind. Patrol your mind by rejecting every thought that doesn't meet the P4:8 standard. Stop it from crossing over into your mind, where it can ruin your relationships and defeat your dreams.

Consider the wisdom we find in Proverbs 4:23: "Above all else, guard your heart, for it is the wellspring of life." Here, the word *heart* is interchangeable with the words *mind* and *soul*, so the writer is stressing that whatever you do, *above all else*, set up a border patrol to guard your mind!

A simple rubber band can help you understand how to patrol your mind. Find a rubber band and put it on your wrist. Snap it with the index finger of your other hand, saying, "I reject this negative thought of _____!" Snap it again and say, "I delete you!" After you apply this exercise enough times, even the mention of a negative thought will become a sore spot in your life!

REJECTING INACCURATE IMAGES FROM OTHERS

A while ago I saw a movie called *Raising Helen*. The main character is a single woman who receives full custody of her sister's children after their parents die in an automobile accident. She enrolls the children in a Christian school, where she meets the pastor who oversees it. They're both single, and immediately there's chemistry between them.

I love the way the movie portrays the pastor. Usually I don't like the way Hollywood depicts Christians or ministers because they appear to be freaks—abnormal and weird. I don't enjoy the spin they place on that role. But in this movie the pastor is a contemporary, normal guy who plays ice hockey and hangs out with his friends. He loves God; he has given his life to Him.

He's attracted to the leading lady in the movie and contemplates how to date her. She won't have anything to do with dating him—she has the religious mind-set that he's a priest who can't get married.

When he says, "You want to go out with me sometime?" She says, "Oh, no! I made you abandon your vows." All he wants is to have dinner and pursue a social relationship. He replies, "Hey, Helen, I'm a Lutheran minister. I can date. I can get married, have children."[5]

As I watched the movie, I liked this guy more and more. I was privately cheering him on because I know many ministers like him. They're great people who aren't stuck back in time. They're living the Christian life right now, relating to a modern and contemporary world. They're rational, intellectual people.

In one scene the minister and the young woman are standing in a doorway. He's talking to her, still trying to convince her to go to dinner with him. She's still nervous about it and putting him off. Finally he takes a step backward and proclaims, "Let me tell you something. I got news for you, little lady. I'm sexy. I'm a sexy man of God, and I know it!"[6]

This man did not internalize someone else's inaccurate image of him! He was saying, "I reject that. You might try to put me in a box, but I know who I am. I may wear this collar, but don't count me out, babe! I'm a man you'd love to spend the rest of your life with!"

You see, you don't have to accept every thought people hold about you or the image they try to project on you. I hope you don't allow people to intimidate you in your workplace because you're a believer. You're the one who's got it going on! If you don't fit into your coworkers' ideas of who you should be because you love God and believe in His moral standard, reject their thoughts!

Over the years Sheila and I have had to fight to develop the kind of church we have now. On a regular basis we have had to reject and resist people's attempts to put us in a religious box. Especially when the church was younger and smaller, people's impressions of church (stained-glass windows and austere organ music) collided with ours. We expect church to be relevant and helpful.

If you stop and ask most people why they don't go to church, they respond with, "*Hello!* It's boring, and it doesn't help me at all." Listen, I believe most people aren't rejecting the good news of the gospel—they're rejecting the *package* it's in.

God has called my wife and me to pastor a church that relates to this generation. Jesus related to His generation. He talked to them in their language of agriculture and shepherding. We talk to our generation in a language they understand.

When people look down on us because of this, we don't allow them to make us feel shallow or like our faith isn't authentic. We know our faith is authentic! We know we love God with all of our hearts, and we know we're committed to His kingdom.

I watched the television coverage of the 2004 Tour de France when Lance Armstrong was close to winning a stage of the race yet wanted one of his teammates to have the opportunity to win it instead. Lance was encouraging him by talking and waving him on. They were just a few kilometers away from the finish line. Lance was slowing down and blocking another racer while telling his USA teammate to go, win a stage.

All of a sudden a racer from another country sped by them and took the lead. Although he was far behind, Lance got that "tiger look" in his eyes, and he started aiming and pedaling. Like a real champion, I could tell he was thinking, "*That's* not going to happen today!"

He stood on his bike and cranked away. He crossed the finish line, one bicycle wheel ahead of his opponent, hands held high in the air! Afterward during an interview he said he wasn't aiming for another win; he just wanted his teammate to be able to win a stage. "He deserved to win," Armstrong said. "He was the man of the day."[7]

When people say, "Everyone's out for themselves— everyone!" you can either accept or reject that thinking. You can buy into that idea, or you can notice people who, like

Lance, go out of their way to do something generous and kind. You will find people like that when you look for them.

The Bible emphasizes that your mind is a battlefield where you win or lose in life. Your life will turn out very differently depending on which thoughts you accept and reject.

KEYS TO REMEMBER

- The Bible emphasizes that your mind is a battlefield where you win or lose in life. Your life will be defined by the thoughts you accept or reject.

- The true north principles at work in the world were established by God, not society.

- The more you live in harmony with God's principles, the better your life will be. You will experience greater joy, greater peace, and greater success.

- Don't give mental energy to a thought unless it passes the P4:8 standard.

- If you want to position yourself for success, you must accept the fact that what you allow into your mind will affect the outcome of your life.

- An unguarded mind is an unprotected mind. Patrol your mind by rejecting every thought that doesn't meet the P4:8 standard.

THINK ABOUT IT

- Do you realize your mind has power to influence and, in some cases, create your reality? What reality can you begin to create through the power of your thoughts?

- Some thoughts are not aligned with God's thoughts. Second Corinthians 10:5 says, "We demolish arguments and every pretension that sets itself up against the knowledge of God, and we take captive every thought to make it obedient to Christ." How can you begin to "take captive every thought" in your life to make it obedient to Christ?

- What is the P4:8 standard? How can you apply it to your life?

- After you decide to focus on only the thoughts that pass the P4:8 standard, set up a border patrol for your mind. This is the action you take to enforce the P4:8 standard. What does your border patrol look like?

CHAPTER 5

REPLACING MIND MONSTERS

N JESUS'S MOST well-known message, the Sermon on the Mount, five of His first few points begin like this: "You have heard that it was said....*But I tell* you."[1] Each time He mentions a commandment from the Old Testament and then expounds on it to take it in a new direction, to elevate the standard.

In doing this, He was saying to the listener and to all of us today that He wants to replace old ways of thinking with a higher way of thinking. The entire sermon emphasizes the futility of trying to do everything on our own. Instead we are called to a higher standard, and we must rely on God's grace to accept it.

You see, mind monsters often invade in the form of ideas, concepts, and philosophies you've picked up along life's way—perhaps in the home you grew up in, or in school from a teacher you admired, at college or work, or from hanging out with friends. When those mind monsters rear their ugly heads, God wants to replace them with His thoughts and His ways.

But how? It seems like the minute we try to *stop* thinking

about something, that very thing consumes our minds. What sort of plan does God have to help us replace mind monsters? There are three steps:

1. Realize that God will help you take control of your mind—you're not on your own!

2. Fill your mind with P4:8 thoughts.

3. Look for wisdom as if there's a reward!

GOD WILL HELP

First of all know that God is *ready* to help you take control of your mind. God *wants* to help free you from thoughts of worry, fear, lust, and anxiety, among other things. He gave you the Bible, which teaches how He thinks—His ideas, perspectives, and thoughts—and how you can think as He does.

One of the greatest promises we have in the Bible is regarding one of the most difficult issues we encounter in our minds: temptation. The apostle Paul wrote, "No temptation has seized you except what is common to man. And God is faithful; he will not let you be tempted beyond what you can bear. But when you are tempted, he will also provide a way out so that you can stand up under it."[2]

Mind monsters will knock on the door of your mind, and they will come in if you let them. Just know that when they do come along, God is right there with you to give you a replacement.

FILL YOUR MIND

God can help you replace mind monsters of negativity when you give Him plenty of *positivity* to work with and partner with Him in the process. So the second thing to know about replacing a mind monster is that you must *fill* your mind every day with thoughts that meet the P4:8 standard. Ask yourself: "Am I full of true, noble, right, pure, lovely, admirable, excellent, and praiseworthy thoughts?"

Businessman W. Clement Stone said, "Keep your mind off the things you don't want by keeping it on the things you do want."[3] The most effective remedy for bad thinking is good thinking. So ask yourself this question: "How often do I think good, faith-based thoughts—focusing on the positive, affirming myself, imagining God doing something good on my behalf, trusting God in every situation, and hoping for the best?"

> *Replace mind monsters by filling your mind every day with thoughts that meet the P4:8 standard.*

If the answer is often—very, very often—then the correlating truth is that there's very little opportunity for negative thoughts to invade your mind. You see, if you're thinking faith-filled thoughts often enough, then a negative invader will be like a car pulling into a shopping mall on Christmas Eve looking for a parking space. It will wander around trying to find a place to park, but all the spaces will be full!

However, if you realize you don't think faith-based thoughts very often, you probably realize you're leaving a lot of space up there that something is going to fill. Whether your mind is a three-deck parking garage or a one-level parking lot, if you fill it every day with thoughts that meet the P4:8 standard, then there will be no space for worry, evil imaginations, fear, discouragement, insecurity, inferiority, and the like.

Do you often find yourself thinking, "I wonder if they like me or not? What do they think of me? I bet they think I'm stupid"? Don't allow space for that! Replace those thoughts with, "What great people I know! I'm sure they're thinking kind thoughts about me."

Even when you've rejected mind monsters, their parking spots will be empty. So they will find their way back in, settling right back into your mind unless you fill their empty spots by thinking differently—by *replacing* the mind-monster thoughts.

TOOLS FOR FILLING YOUR MIND

Stock up on some tools that help you fill your mind with good things, such as a Bible you will actually read (and understand) or uplifting audio (such as CDs and MP3s of praise and worship music, other positive music, preaching, and so on). The Bible is available in so many great translations these days it has never been easier to find one you'll understand and enjoy reading. The same goes for Christian music—whatever style of music you enjoy listening to, the chances are good that you can find something uplifting and Scripture-based in that genre.

Another great idea is to memorize a scripture a month. (You'll find several great ones in Appendix A.) Choose a verse and memorize it. Say it over and over again. Repetition is what helps you deposit it into your memory bank. After a year, you'll have twelve of them stored up. After two years, you'll have twenty-four. A few years of memorizing the Word will fill the spaces of your conscious and subconscious mind.

My wife fills our house with music. As she moves from one area to another in our home, she listens to different radio or cable TV stations. It never occurs to her that I walk through the house and get totally confused. I'll find myself in the middle of an upbeat song, then walk to the other end of the house and hear something slow and therapeutic. But she's filling up every square inch of the house with something good and positive.

Another great way to fill your mind with good things is through prayer, and one of the best examples we have of prayer can be found in Matthew 6:9–13, the well-known Lord's Prayer: "Our Father in heaven, hallowed be Your name. Your kingdom come. Your will be done on earth as it is in heaven. Give us this day our daily bread. And forgive us our debts, as we forgive our debtors. And do not lead us into temptation, but deliver us from the evil one. For Yours is the kingdom and the power and the glory forever. Amen" (NKJV).

This is a perfect model for prayer, and you can remember it with five "P" words: praise, plan, provision, purification, and protection.

Begin with *praise*.

"Our Father in heaven, hallowed be Your name..."

When you pray, begin by directing your words to God, praising Him for who He is, what He's done in your life, and what He can do. You can thank God for who He is by learning some of His names. In Exodus 3 God tells Moses to tell them, "I AM has sent me to you."[4] God wants us to know that He is both noun and verb—He functions as anything and everything we could ever imagine, ask for, think of, or need.

He also gives us some specific names throughout the Bible. Some powerful and well-known names are the Jehovah compound names that originated in the Hebrew language. Here are a few examples:

- *Jehovah-Jireh*: the Lord God my provider[5]

- *Jehovah-T'sidkenu*: the Lord God my righteousness[6]

- *Jehovah-Rapha*: the Lord God my healer[7]

- *Jehovah-Nissi*: the Lord God my banner[8]

- *Jehovah-Shalom*: the Lord God my peace[9]

Let's approach God with grateful hearts and thanksgiving when we begin to pray.

Pray God's *plan*.

"Your kingdom come. Your will be done on earth as it is in heaven."

Pray that God will accomplish His purposes in the various people in your world. Take an opportunity to pray for your family, your church, your friends, and your coworkers. This is also a good place to pray for government leaders—local, regional, national, and even global. You and I can pray God's plan for our own lives and anyone else we can think of.

Pray God's *provision*.

"Give us this day our daily bread."

God wants us to bring all of our requests to Him. He wants us to see Him as our provider and ask Him not only for our needs but also the desires of hearts. Pray for the things you need God's help or resources in—food and shelter, fresh ideas, open doors of opportunities, finances and wisdom, more networked relationships. Whatever you can ask for, bring it before God. When we bring it before God and acknowledge Him as our provider, then when that prayer is answered, we can turn it around into *praise* and thank Him for meeting our needs!

Pray for *purification*.

"And forgive us our debts, as we forgive our debtors."

We are human, so chances are things will happen every single day that we can bring to God and ask His forgiveness for. A prayer for purification can be as simple as, "Forgive me of all my sin." Pray for God to forgive you of your own sin, and pray that you are able to forgive yourself and others. Sometimes people hold on to unforgiveness toward others (or even themselves) and allow bitterness to grow in their lives. By practicing this step on a consistent basis you will continually prevent bitterness from taking root and developing into deeper things, such as hatred, envy, or pride.

Pray the *protection* of God.

"And do not lead us into temptation, but deliver us from the evil one."

Pray specifically for God's wisdom and direction as you take the next steps of life. God wants the best for you. Sometimes we just have to get out of our own way and allow God to be at work in our lives. Pray for His protection in new ventures, new relationships, your decisions, and your future. When our daughter, Jodi, was a little girl, my wife and I used to pray most nights when we put her to bed that God would station His angels all around our family.

Ask God for wisdom, and He will give it to you. (You will read more about wisdom in a couple of pages.) And ask for protection, and you can be assured that Romans 8:28 will be true for you—all things work together for the good of those who love Christ.

Finally, return to *praise*.

"For Yours is the kingdom and the power and the glory forever. Amen."

Praise God once more for who He is, declaring your faith in God's promises with a spirit of thanksgiving. Use your words to take dominion over your life, your circumstances, and your future. Praise God for wanting His best for you.

Reading your Bible, memorizing Scripture, listening to positive audio, praying biblically—these are all great ways to fill your mind with good things!

THE REWARD OF WISDOM

The last step in replacing mind monsters is to look for wisdom as if there's a reward for finding it—because there is one! Proverbs 9:12 says, "If you are wise, your wisdom will reward you."

It's just as easy to be wise as it is to be foolish—it's all in the choices you make. The price to obtain wisdom may be higher, but wisdom will do much to improve your performance in life.

When you pull your car into a filling station, you select the octane level of the gas you're going to put into the fuel tank. You can choose a low grade or a high grade. A high-performance automobile uses high-grade fuel because that will cause it to perform better. In much the same way you will perform better in life if you choose to be wise.

Wisdom is available if you seek it. God doesn't hide wisdom and say, "Too bad! I hope you can find it!" If you've never read Proverbs 1–3, I recommend you do. It tells you that wisdom can be found; it's not hiding. Wisdom practically stands on the street corner and yells out to you. God is longing to give you wisdom. You just have to ask for it.

There is one important distinction to make, though: wisdom is not the same thing as education. That's why someone can earn a counseling degree and author a book on marriage but then get divorced, while a simple couple with only an eighth-grade education can have a fantastic life together.

Wisdom was God's first creation. The Bible says wisdom was the craftsman of the universe, meaning the entire universe was formed by wisdom.[10] So the more you agree with wisdom, the more you act in wisdom, the better your life will be—less heartache, less crisis, less turmoil.

The Bible says that what wisdom provides is greater than silver.[11] If you take time to hear her voice, she will speak to you. Wisdom is God-given, and in order to get it, all you have to is ask Him for it.[12] It really is as simple as that!

RIGHT AND WRONG VS. WISE AND UNWISE

Sometimes we have to consider much more than whether a decision is simply right or wrong. We have to consider whether it is wise or unwise. Why? Lend me your imagination for a moment.

Imagine a room full of furniture, absolutely crowded with couches, chairs, coffee tables, end tables, lamps, even pictures on the wall. Throw a piano in there if you want. Do you have your mental picture? Now I want you to imagine string winding through all that furniture, interconnecting it.

In some cases maybe a piece of string will only tie the leg of the coat rack to a bookshelf, and in other cases, a single string may wrap around the loveseat, behind the framed family photo, through the rug, and up to the curtain rod. You get the idea. Now that you have your fully furnished, fully interconnected room, I want you to imagine what would happen if you decided to move even one piece of furniture.

This is the complex world we live in, where our decisions, like it or not, affect someone or something. This is where we have to think not just about decisions being right or wrong but also wise or unwise. It may be a good idea—a right idea—to move that table lamp from one end of the couch to the other, but in so doing you might knock three pictures off the wall.

Wisdom allows us to actively and skillfully think through the decision and determine ways to make the right choice without suffering losses. Wisdom helps us think things through and see the deeper ramifications of our actions.

WISDOM VS. SOCIETY

Welcome wisdom. Want wisdom. The world has its own way of thinking. The world has its own ideas. As you walk through life, you have to be careful not to copy the decision-making instincts of society.

You have to say, "Wait just a minute. I recognize a mind monster getting into my psyche, leading me down a road of destruction, and I can't afford to think that way. I have to elevate my mind to a higher way of thinking. I don't have to fear that no one's going to want me. I don't have to fear that I'm going to live the rest of my life alone. I can focus on the positive and affirm myself. I can imagine God doing something good, and I can trust God even now while I'm single. I will hope for the best in my life and future."

When negative information tempts your mind, declare: "I reject you. You can be replaced because you're not produced from faith. You're from fear and doubt. Many have walked down your pathway and have ended up in major crises. I'm going to choose the path of wisdom. The price might be a little higher, but I'm going to go for the high-octane stuff because I want a better life."

Jesus loved to talk about wisdom. He said, "A foolish man

builds a house on the sand, and when the storms of life come, the house collapses. But a wise man builds his house on a solid foundation, and when the wind blows and the storm comes, the house stands firm."[13] Jesus wasn't talking about a physical house. He was talking about the life you build.

He's encouraging you to build your life on wise thoughts. Watch for wisdom; fill your day with it. Instead of being drawn toward negative invaders of the mind, don't allow space for them.

Listen for someone to say something wise. Write it down; memorize it. Say it over and over, adding, "Oh, that's good. I'm going to keep that close to my heart. I'm going to put that in my mind. I'm going to build up an inventory of wisdom inside me so wisdom flows out of my life like a river. When I have a decision to make, I'm going to make a wise choice, not a foolish one. I will be full of wisdom."

I love the story a friend of mine named Joseph Garlington tells. He said a university professor was computing grades at the end of a semester. A female student approached him the night before the grades were to be released. Walking into his office wearing a tight white top, she perched herself seductively on his desk and whispered, "What can I do to get a good grade?" The professor, a man of God, threw her out of his office and ran home!

As soon as he stepped inside the door, he called out for his wife: "Come here. Go to the bedroom, put on a white T-shirt, and walk down these steps. I have a thought I've got to get out of my mind, and I want to replace it with a better one!"

When some men try to overcome lust, they stay focused

on the very images they want to get out of their mind. Even though they want to get that woman out of their mind, they approach it in a way that keeps her in there.

They say, "I won't think about that woman. I'm not going to think about her. I rebuke that thought. I rebuke that woman!" And they just remain stuck on the thought they're trying to reject! What are they doing all week? They're thinking about the woman. But the professor in this story understood the secret of replacing a mind monster with a positive thought.

So to recap, the first step in getting rid of a mind monster is to recognize it. Then you must reject it, and afterward, replace it with a thought of faith and confidence. Next I'll show you how to retrain your mind to become the person you aspire to be.

KEYS TO REMEMBER

- Realize that God will help you take control of your mind—you're not on your own!

- Fill your mind with P4:8 thoughts so there is no space left for mind monsters.

- Look for wisdom as if there's a reward.

- Recognize that wisdom is available if you seek it.

- Think not only about decisions being right or wrong but also whether they are wise or unwise.

THINK ABOUT IT

- Ask yourself: "Am I full of true, noble, right, pure, lovely, admirable, excellent, and praiseworthy thoughts?" If the answer is no or not often, then how can you increase those types of thoughts in your life?

- Think about how often you think good, faith-based thoughts—focusing on the positive, affirming yourself, imagining God doing something good on your behalf, trusting God in every situation, and hoping for the best. Are there ways you can nurture faith-based thoughts? Is there a situation in your life right now that you need to focus good, faith-based thoughts toward?

- Consider making a replacement chart. In one column, write statements you find yourself saying (or thinking) often, and in the next column write a replacement phrase. For example, insecurity and doubt live in statements such as, "I wonder if they like me or not. What do they think of me?" Replace those thoughts with, "What great people I know! I'm sure they're thinking kind thoughts about me."

CHAPTER 6

RETRAINING YOUR MIND

COMPUTERS SEEM TO be everywhere today—in homes, offices, and even cars. How a computer works is similar to how your mind works.

My automobile has a computer that tells me when I have a flat tire. After Sunday service during one of our church conferences, my wife and I took some of our guest pastors out to lunch. On our way to the restaurant, my dashboard illuminated two words: flat tire!

Immediately I felt anxious. Glancing over at Sheila, I exclaimed, "Great! What a time for a flat tire. Can you believe it?"

I apologized to the people in the backseat as my mind reeled: "Why do I have a flat tire now? Why did it happen on a Sunday when I happen to be wearing a suit? Why couldn't this happen another time?"

Suddenly another thought occurred to me: "Maybe I can make it to the restaurant and call a tow truck." We made it! I hurried out of the car to examine the tires. They all looked good—everything was fine. We shrugged and walked inside the restaurant.

Halfway through our meal, one of the men in our group left to check the tires. When he reappeared, he said the tires looked great. He commented that it looked like there was no problem at all.

When we finished our meal, we started the car to head home. Immediately the dashboard blazed: flat tire, flat tire, flat tire!

Now no one in his right mind could ever accuse me of being a handyman, but in this situation I knew what to do. When I arrived home, I pulled out my tire pressure gauge. Yes, being the handyman I am, I checked the pressure in all of the tires. And it was fine! So I walked inside the house and waited to see what would happen in the morning.

On Monday morning I examined the tires again. They all looked fine. As I headed for the office, the infamous red light announced: flat tire, flat tire, flat tire! At that moment I recognized what was going on. I said to myself, "My car has a mind monster, and I know exactly what to do!"

In a gesture of fun, I announced, "I *recognize* you! I *reject* you! My tire's not flat. You're a liar!" I continued, "I *replace* you—I'm going to override you right now. I'm going to act like you don't exist. I'm going to keep driving to the office. I'm going to keep riding in this car. Nothing is wrong."

I made it to the office, and I made it back home. On Tuesday the car made it everywhere I needed to go. All week long the car made it everywhere I had to go, and all week long that red dashboard light lied to me.

Every time I heard new passengers gasp at the warning light, I applied the three Rs: "I recognize you. I reject you.

I replace you." I explained to my companions, "Don't worry about it. The message is wrong. It's a mind monster! It doesn't know what it's talking about. Just agree with me that everything's fine."

On Friday I took the car to the shop and explained to the mechanic, "The mind of my car isn't functioning right. Would you please reprogram it?" He did just that—he retrained the computer in my car, and it hasn't lied to me since!

Retrain your mind. To get rid of a mind monster, recognize it, reject it, replace it, and then retrain your mind to think differently.

RETRAINING YOUR MIND: HERE'S HOW

How do you retrain your mind? First realize that your mind automatically thinks in habitual patterns. In other words, your mind is a creature of habit. The brain cells of your computer (mind) record each step of your decisions in order to repeat them. Do you notice that you dress the same way every morning? When you put on your pants, notice that you begin with the same foot every day.

This is because your brain has recorded each dressing step as a "habit." It can be a scary thing to drive all the way home from work and realize you weren't consciously aware of the road or traffic. Pulling into your driveway, all of a sudden you realize, "Oh, I'm home!" You made every turn, stopped at every light, and didn't run anyone off the road. Your subconscious mind worked for you and brought you home that day.

That's the power of the human mind. But you have to realize that God created it to work for your good, not to work against you. Show your mind what to do, and it will automatically begin to form a habit. Unfortunately many times this same great mind picks up a negative train of thought and falls into a rut of habitual worry, doubt, fear, skepticism, or criticism. Your mind will remain this way until you consciously make an effort to reprogram it.

I remember going horseback riding as a child when my parents took us to one of those trail-riding stables. It didn't take long for me to realize it was *boring*! When I wanted the horse to run or veer off the beaten path a little, I would command, "Giddy up!" I would kick the horse or pull on the reins, but that horse would just stay right there on the same old familiar trail. I caught on quickly that this horse was doing nothing except following the others in a line and going down the same trail as always.

Your mind automatically thinks in habitual patterns.
In other words, your mind is a creature of habit.

Your mind works in much the same way. Just as it takes a determined effort, a strong will, and authority to make a trail horse turn off the beaten path ("Horse, we're not going down this trail right now. I'm your master, and we're going over here"), it also takes authority to take your mind down a new trail.

In other words, it's one thing to recognize, reject, and replace mind monsters. But you must also retrain your mind by continually repeating the process! Keep recognizing, keep rejecting, and keep replacing them. You can't expect to have a different mind-set within twenty-four hours or even forty-eight. Some psychologists say it takes a minimum of eleven days—others say at least twenty-one days—to create a new habit.[1]

After my family moved to a new home, I left the office one day and drove all the way to our former house before I realized I didn't live there anymore! Your mind develops a mental rut and dictates your direction. Your mind will stay on that same, familiar trail of thought until you interrupt the old pattern and consciously say, "I'm going to retrain you to think a new and better way."

How much energy do you expend on mind monsters that jump into your life, taking you down trails where you don't want to go? Consider Doris's story. After work one day, she sat down with her husband and said, "I have to talk to you. Something's really bothering me." She continued, "I have cancer."

Shocked, he said, "What do you mean you have cancer? Did the doctor examine you?"

She said, "No, but my boss died of cancer, and I remember the evolution of the disease. He had headaches, and I've had headaches for the last few days. He said his lips started turning numb, and this morning on my way to work my lips were turning numb."

At this point, her husband broke out in laughter. Of course, that wasn't the response she expected. Feeling frustrated, she burst out, "Why are you laughing? This isn't funny. *This isn't funny—I have cancer!* Do you understand?"

By this time he was in a ball of stitches, laughing up a storm. Finally she demanded, "What's wrong!"

Composing himself, he explained, "Honey, before you left for work this morning, do you remember we kissed good-bye?"

"Yes," she replied.

He continued, "Well, I had just applied numbing medication to my lip for a fever blister!" (Doris was speechless for a while!)

Maybe that story isn't funny to you because you or someone you love really *does* have cancer. Or maybe you're facing some other big challenge. Maybe you don't know how you're going to feed your family today. Maybe you have a dangerously rebellious child. Maybe you have some secret sin that you just can't seem to conquer, no matter how hard you try.

The list goes on and on, and in each of those instances, I say to you all the more: you need God's help to fight the battle against mind monsters. He hasn't given you "a spirit of fear, but of power and of love and of a sound mind."[2] Your mind is as much a battleground as the real world is. And just as it takes time and effort to allow a mind monster to master your thoughts, so does it take time and effort to master a new positive mental habit. Which way do you choose to live?

RETRAIN YOUR MIND TO SEE GOD AT WORK

Do you remember the vacation I mentioned earlier that ended with me in a hospital in Bermuda? (Sheila and I were in a motorbike accident on a major thoroughfare in Bermuda. She walked away with only a few minor scrapes, but I was glued to the pavement with a fractured pelvis.)

In life sometimes things just happen. Not every bad thing is caused by the devil. Satan didn't cause my accident in Bermuda. The combination of inexperienced riders, narrow roads, left-side-of-the-road driving, fast-moving traffic, and bad judgment equaled a disaster waiting to happen. Sometimes the recipes of life include some not-so-good things. However, in those times, if you train your eyes (and your mind) to look for God, you will see that He is still at work.

Here's how we found God working on our behalf in that situation:

- We didn't go over the edge of the road or under the guardrail and tumble down a steep cliff.

- A group of police officers happened to be in the area jogging in a training exercise when the accident took place. Within minutes they had the accident scene under control, and a couple of them even joined my daughter and wife in prayer!

- The driver behind us had a cell phone for an officer to use.

- The only hospital on the island was just a couple minutes away (people often bleed to death from pelvis fractures).

- At the hospital in Bermuda, I had a private room with a view of the ocean.

- One of the nurses had a daughter who attended our church in Seattle, and the daughter had been praying that her mother would come to know God.

- We left the island two days before the worst storm in fifty years occurred.

- My pelvis healed without surgery, and there was no long-term damage.

These are just a few of the ways we recognized God at work in that situation. Sometimes circumstances in our lives don't look good. There were some scary moments throughout that season for our family, but we kept looking for God at work, and in the end we saw that He really did work all things together for the good.

When experiences touch our lives, they don't always feel good. But as they get mixed into God's bigger plan for our lives, we can begin to see that He really does work everything together for our good. That is why it is so important to retrain our mind to look for God at work. Chances are He is working behind the scenes in the middle of a disaster, even though we can't see Him.

WHO DO YOU WANT TO BE?

Have you ever thought much about your habits (observable tendencies and characteristics that form your behavior patterns)? Have you ever noticed that when people watch you, they notice your habits and then describe you that way? How do you want to be described? *Who do you really want to be?*

Some people are described as funny. They are always finding humor in everything. When you're around them, you expect to laugh a lot. They're funny because their mind is programmed that way. They probably received a few laughs when they were young. They enjoyed bringing pleasure to people, and consequently their mind picked up on that train of thought. Now they're witty and amusing, and we call them funny.

Then there are other people who find humor in nothing. People describe them as sad, gloomy, or negative. Others aren't funny, but they're not depressing either. About them we might say, "They're the most upbeat, positive person you'll ever want to meet."

A young man commented to me, "I know my father is going to be angry with me." I thought to myself, "How does he know that? How can he predict that?" But then I quickly realized, "His conclusion has to be based on past experience." The father behaved in a predictable pattern of anger.

Why do we describe people as funny, sad, or angry? Because they *are* that way—habitually and automatically!

Decide and declare what kind of person you want to be and direct your mind toward that goal. A science called "neuro-linguistic programming"—*neuro* meaning "brain" and *linguistic* meaning "language"—verifies the Bible's teaching that your mind and your words work together to create thinking patterns.

As strange as it may sound, most people don't think about what kind of person they want to become—they just become what they become. They accept the first thought that enters their mind and allow it shape them.

They subconsciously conform to the thinking pattern of the world. Rather than deciding and declaring what kind of person they want to be, they allow their surroundings to mold them.

I know people who say, "You don't understand my life. You don't understand what has happened to me." Sometimes people use their circumstances to excuse their negative mindset. They justify living in worry, intimidation, and fear. Have you used the events and circumstances of your life to justify staying on the same negative trail of thought?

If you drive down an old logging trail or dirt road in the Great Northwest, often your tires will bump along the ruts in the road. Sometimes they are so deep vehicles get stuck and have a hard time getting out.

Likewise you can get stuck in the deep mental ruts that reach into and take over your patterns of thinking. To get "unstuck," you have to be willing as a child of God to take Romans 12:2 as your own: "Do not conform any longer to the [thinking] pattern of this world, but be transformed by the renewing of your mind."

The apostle Paul is clearly saying there is a right way to think. If you partner with God and renew your mind, you *will be* transformed!

In other words, don't let the old trail dictate how you will think—carve out a new trail! Don't allow your mind to take you down the familiar, easy road it has memorized after going through mental rut territory. Interrupt those negative thoughts—recognize, reject, and replace them until your negative habits disappear. Retrain your brain to embrace new habits by deciding whom you want to become, declaring it, and renewing your mind with the Word of God until you become the person you want to be.

Do you wonder if this really works? Consider how retraining the mind lowers the repeat offender rate of former prisoners in the United States. The world's largest prison population per capita resides in the United States. There are more people incarcerated in the United States than in any other nation in the world (more than 2.25 *million* people at the end of 2009, according to the US Bureau of Justice Statistics).[3] Unfortunately, there's not a lot of hope for them, even after they're released, because studies show inmates have more than a 50 percent chance of returning to prison for a similar offense.[4]

In response to this, faith-based prison programs have launched in the last few years, with the first all faith-based prison opening in Florida. Convicted people can decide not to go there; however, the prison has all they can handle because so many people *want* to go there.

Why? They're experiencing great results! The reoffender rate has decreased significantly in these prisons. And because you can't argue with the results, this program has overflowed into other states.[5]

In these prisons, the lifestyle is geared toward faith. Prisoners attend worship services where they praise and worship God. They encourage each other. The employees are believers, so when prisoners find themselves at a crossroads in life, they pray about it together. They read the Scriptures daily and apply them by faith.

The inmates encourage one another in their faith. As a result prisoners are leaving this system with the hope they won't return because they have retrained their minds. They're thinking in a new way. They've found a way to get out of the old mental rut.

Why wait until you're facing divorce? Why wait until you encounter a huge financial crisis? Why wait until you do something in a fit of anger that lands you in a prison cell? Why not begin today to retrain your mind?

Benjamin Franklin, a great hero and leader in our nation, understood this principle. As a young man, he wrote down thirteen virtues he wanted to exemplify. He focused on one virtue each week, with the goal of absorbing that virtue into his behavior. In thirteen weeks' time he cycled through all the virtues on his piece of paper. He repeated this sequence four times each year.

I think it's exciting to read about this famous man who took the responsible step of gathering a piece of paper and a writing instrument; then writing down virtues that essentially proclaimed, "This is the kind of man I want to be."[6] Benjamin Franklin understood that to become a better person, he must lead his mind down a new trail of habitual thought.

As a person who desires a new life and a new future, you can't afford certain habitual thoughts to remain in your mind. For the sake of your future, your loved ones, and your legacy, choose to change thoughts currently programmed into your mind that block your way to a better life.

Writing down who you want to be may sound trivial to you, but trust me—it activates change! I invite you right now to write down three words, maybe five if you're feeling motivated, that describe the kind of person you want to be.

Don't take this lightly. Think to the highest level of your ambitions, all the way to the desires you know God is putting into your heart. This is not a spooky, mysterious exercise. I believe you know who God wants you to be; all you're doing is declaring it! Have confidence in knowing your highest and best aspirations are in alignment with God's plan for your life.

The person I want to be is:

1. _____

2. _____

3. _____

4. _____

5. _____

What kind of characteristics did you write down? Happy, generous, hospitable, positive? Encouraging, obedient, strong, influential, trustworthy, consistent? I bet you didn't write: negative, discouraging, anxious, unhappy, mad.

Do you know why? Because God created you to reach for the higher good. He created you to aspire to new levels. Something inside every single person, even a person incarcerated today who feels like he or she really messed up, says, "Wait. It's not over until it's over. I can be the person God wants me to be. I can change my old ways and become a brand-new person."

When you take the time to actually write virtues down, or memorize the F.A.I.T.H. acronym and implement the principles every day, you're moving down a new trail, leading yourself in a new direction.

The Bible says, "If anyone is in Christ, he is a new creation; the old has gone, the new has come!"[7] And remember Ephesians 4:23: "Be made new in the attitude of your minds." The Bible talks about newness. The Bible talks about change. The Bible talks about transformation, and I think many people get the idea that it's a passive thing, that it's all up to God. What I want to help you understand today is that you must partner with God. You must decide what kind of person you really want to be and then accomplish it.

Would you like to change your life and your future to have the best life you can live? You can! With faith and the P4:8 standard (and a rubber band, if needed), you can recognize, reject, and replace mind monsters that steal your life. You can retrain your mind to automatically think a new, better way. You can decide and say who you want to become and keep a fresh mental attitude by incorporating God's thoughts into your daily routine.

KEYS TO REMEMBER

- Your mind thinks in habitual patterns.

- Show your mind what to do, and it will automatically begin to develop a new habitual pattern of thinking.

- It is possible to get stuck in deep mental ruts that take over patterns of thinking.

- As a person who desires a new life, a new future, and a new legacy, you can't afford certain habitual thoughts to remain in your mind.

- Choose to change thoughts currently programmed in your mind that block your way to a better life.

- With faith and the P4:8 standard (and a rubber band, if needed), you can recognize, reject, and replace mind monsters that steal your life.

THINK ABOUT IT

- Consider writing virtues down (just as Benjamin Franklin did) or memorize the F.A.I.T.H. acronym, and implement one virtue or principle every day. The action and investment of your time (and your mind) will lead you in a new and better direction.

- What principles can you use to retrain your thought patterns to live the best life possible?

- Do you notice that each day you live your life through a series of learned habits (for example, how you brush your teeth)? In the same way can you identify habits of thinking by recalling the last few weeks? How can you begin to change your thinking habits for the future?

- If someone watched your habits and then described what was observed, what do you think they would say about you? Is that who you really want to be?

- Have you ever justified a negative thought by blaming the events and the circumstances of your life? Sometimes people justify living in worry, intimidation, and fear. What are some ways you can retrain your mind to think differently instead of justifying your current thinking patterns?

- If you haven't already done so while reading this chapter, take some time write down three to five words that describe the kind of person you want to be.

CHAPTER 7

THE PERSON YOU
WANT TO BE

N 2006 JOURNALIST Joshua Foer was sent to cover a little
event called the USA Memory Championships, an annual
competition to see who among the participants has the best
memory. There are a variety of events, such as memorizing
strings of random numbers or lines of poetry. There is even
one event in which the "mental athlete" (the participants' pre-
ferred terminology) must memorize the order of a deck of
cards as quickly as he can.

Foer expected to find a collection of people with supe-
rior brain skills, participants who were genetically gifted to
have great, competitive-level memories. Instead he found a
random bunch of ordinary people. As he spoke with the different mental athletes, he began to hear over and over again
that there was nothing special about them and that anyone
could compete in such an event. Even him.

So Foer accepted the challenge and began a yearlong
training regimen to prepare himself to compete in the following year's competition. The key, he was told, was in
learning to think differently. Foer learned that his memory

was already a good one. He just hadn't been using it, hadn't been developing it, hadn't been training it. If he could just change the way he thought, he could compete.

> *Writing down the kind of person*
> *you want to be activates change.*

And so Foer dove into his new obsession. He followed the steps. He sought out wise counsel from people who had expanded their memory's capacity. And he did the hard, grueling work of challenging himself. One year later Foer surprised everyone—including himself—when he set a new American record by memorizing the order of a complete deck of cards in one minute forty seconds.[1]

My prayer as you complete this book is that you exceed Joshua Foer. He conquered mind monsters to win a competition. I want you to win in life. I hope you come away feeling good about the tools you have at your disposal to defeat negative invaders of the mind.

The fact of the matter is that God loves you so much He accepts you just the way you are. But He also loves you too much to let you *stay* that way. He has amazing plans for your life and has given you the talents, the skills, and the opportunities to live out those plans.

Through God's Word and with His strength you can recognize mind monsters in your life, reject them, replace them, and then retrain your mind to live without them. With God, you can become the person you want to be!

KEYS TO REMEMBER

- Learning to think differently will change the outcome of your life.

- God loves you so much that He accepts you just the way you are—but He also loves you too much to let you stay that way.

- With God you can become the person you want to be!

THINK ABOUT IT

- What is an area you need to think differently about in order to go to the next level in your life, your relationships, your job, etc.?

- What have you learned about God and His love after reading this book?

- What are the four Rs we mentioned in the last few chapters? How can you incorporate them into your everyday life?

- How do you intend to partner with God to recognize mind monsters and replace them with good, faith-based thoughts?

SCRIPTURES TO BUILD F.A.I.T.H.

FOCUS ON THE POSITIVE

Now to him who is able to do immeasurably more than all we ask or imagine, according to his power that is at work within us, to him be glory in the church and in Christ Jesus throughout all generations, for ever and ever! Amen.

—Ephesians 3:20–21

Finally, brothers, whatever is true, whatever is noble, whatever is right, whatever is pure, whatever is lovely, whatever is admirable—if anything is excellent or praiseworthy—think about such things.

—Philippians 4:8

Be constantly renewed in the spirit of your mind [having a fresh mental and spiritual attitude].

—Ephesians 4:23, AMP

Blessed is the man who does not walk in the counsel of the wicked or stand in the way of sinners or sit in the seat of mockers. But his delight is in the law of the Lord, and on his law he meditates day and night. He is like a tree planted by streams of water, which yields its fruit in season and whose leaf does not wither. Whatever he does prospers.

—Psalm 1:1–3

The weapons we fight with are not the weapons of the world. On the contrary, they have divine power to demolish strongholds. We demolish arguments and every pretension that sets itself up against the knowledge of God, and we take captive every thought to make it obedient to Christ.

—2 Corinthians 10:4–5

We are hard pressed on every side, but not crushed; perplexed, but not in despair; persecuted, but not abandoned; struck down, but not destroyed.

—2 Corinthians 4:8–9

AFFIRM YOURSELF

If God is for us, who can be against us?

—Romans 8:31

Those who receive God's abundant provision of grace and of the gift of righteousness reign in life.

—Romans 5:17

Being confident of this, that he who began a good work in you will carry it on to completion until the day of Christ Jesus.

—Philippians 1:6

Do not conform any longer to the pattern of this world, but be transformed by the renewing of your mind. Then you will be able to test and approve what God's will is—his good, pleasing and perfect will.

—ROMANS 12:2

I can do all things through Christ who strengthens me.

—PHILIPPIANS 4:13, NKJV

Now if we are children, then we are heirs—heirs of God and co-heirs with Christ, if indeed we share in his sufferings in order that we may also share in his glory.

—ROMANS 8:17

We are more than conquerors through him who loved us. For I am convinced that neither death nor life, neither angels nor demons, neither the present nor the future, nor any powers, neither height nor depth, nor anything else in all creation, will be able to separate us from the love of God that is in Christ Jesus our Lord.

—ROMANS 8:37–39

If anyone is in Christ, he is a new creation; the old has gone, the new has come!

—2 CORINTHIANS 5:17

IMAGINE GOD DOING SOMETHING GOOD IN YOUR SITUATION

I am still confident of this: I will see the goodness of the LORD in the land of the living.

—PSALM 27:13

No eye has seen, no ear has heard, no mind has conceived what God has prepared for those who love him.

—1 CORINTHIANS 2:9

He who was seated on the throne said, "I am making everything new!"

—REVELATION 21:5

And we know that in all things God works for the good of those who love him, who have been called according to his purpose.

—ROMANS 8:28

My word that goes out from my mouth...will not return to me empty, but will accomplish what I desire and achieve the purpose for which I sent it.

—ISAIAH 55:11

For he will command his angels concerning you to guard you in all your ways.

—PSALM 91:11

TRUST GOD IN ALL THINGS

You will keep in perfect peace him whose mind is steadfast, because he trusts in you.

—ISAIAH 26:3

He who trusts in himself is a fool, but he who walks in wisdom is kept safe.

—PROVERBS 28:26

"For my thoughts are not your thoughts, neither are your ways my ways," declares the LORD. "As the heavens are higher than the earth, so are my ways higher than your ways and my thoughts than your thoughts."

—ISAIAH 55:8–9

Without faith it is impossible to please God, because anyone who comes to him must believe that he exists and that he rewards those who earnestly seek him.

—HEBREWS 11:6

We know and rely on the love God has for us. God is love. Whoever lives in love lives in God, and God in him.

—1 JOHN 4:16

But the Lord is faithful, and he will strengthen and protect you from the evil one.

—2 THESSALONIANS 3:3

He is the Rock, his works are perfect, and all his ways are just. A faithful God who does no wrong, upright and just is he.

—DEUTERONOMY 32:4

Not that we are competent in ourselves to claim anything for ourselves, but our competence comes from God.

—2 CORINTHIANS 3:5

He who trusts in the LORD will prosper.

—PROVERBS 28:25

HOPE FOR THE BEST

Faith is being sure of what we hope for and certain of what we do not see.

—HEBREWS 11:1

Therefore, preparing your minds for action, and being sober-minded, set your hope fully on the grace that will be brought to you at the revelation of Jesus Christ.

—1 PETER 1:13, ESV

May the God of hope fill you with all joy and peace as you trust in him, so that you may overflow with hope by the power of the Holy Spirit.

—ROMANS 15:13

For I am the LORD, your God, who takes hold of your right hand and says to you, do not fear; I will help you.

—ISAIAH 41:13

I pray also that the eyes of your heart may be enlightened in order that you may know the hope to which he has called you, the riches of his glorious inheritance in the saints, and his incomparably great power for us who believe.

—EPHESIANS 1:18–19

Those who have faith are blessed along with Abraham, the man of faith.

—GALATIANS 3:9

But seek first his kingdom and his righteousness, and all these things will be given to you as well.

—MATTHEW 6:33

Jesus looked at them and said, "With man this is impossible, but not with God; all things are possible with God."

—MARK 10:27

Praise be to the God and Father of our Lord Jesus Christ, who has blessed us in the heavenly realms with every spiritual blessing in Christ.

—EPHESIANS 1:3

FEED FAITH, STARVE FEAR

So we fix our eyes not on what is seen, but on what is unseen. For what is seen is temporary, but what is unseen is eternal.

—2 CORINTHIANS 4:18

But we have this treasure in jars of clay to show that this all-surpassing power is from God and not from us.

—2 CORINTHIANS 4:7

It is written: "I believed; therefore I have spoken." With that same spirit of faith we also believe and therefore speak.

—2 CORINTHIANS 4:13

Be strong and courageous. Do not be terrified; do not be discouraged, for the LORD your God will be with you wherever you go.

—JOSHUA 1:9

If any of you lacks wisdom, he should ask God, who gives generously to all without finding fault, and it will be given to him. But when he asks, he must believe and not doubt, because he who doubts is like a wave of the sea, blown and tossed by the wind. That man should not think he will receive anything from the Lord; he is a double-minded man, unstable in all he does.

—JAMES 1:5–8

Cast all your anxiety on him because he cares for you.

—1 PETER 5:7

So do not fear, for I am with you; do not be dismayed, for I am your God. I will strengthen you and help you; I will uphold you with my righteous right hand.

—ISAIAH 41:10

Do not be anxious about anything, but in everything, by prayer and petition, with thanksgiving, present your requests to God. And the peace of God, which transcends all understanding, will guard your hearts and your minds in Christ Jesus.

—PHILIPPIANS 4:6–7

There is no fear in love. But perfect love drives out fear, because fear has to do with punishment. The one who fears is not made perfect in love.

—1 JOHN 4:18

Therefore I tell you, do not worry about your life, what you will eat or drink; or about your body, what you will wear. Is not life more important than food, and the body more important than clothes? Look at the birds of the air; they do not sow or reap or store away in barns, and yet your heavenly Father feeds them. Are you not much more valuable than they?

—MATTHEW 6:25–26

DECLARATIONS TO CONQUER MIND MONSTERS

I have the mind of Christ. I choose to take a stand against mind monsters.[1]

I choose to have a positive mind with positive thoughts. I will think on things that are true, noble, right, pure, lovely, admirable, excellent, or praiseworthy.[2]

I have hidden God's Word in my heart that I might not sin against Him.[3]

I will look for wisdom as if there's a reward for it.[4]

God is with me always, even to the end of the age, He will meet all my needs.[5]

I will recognize mind monsters by paying attention to my internal dialogue, moods, and conversation.

I choose to change thoughts programmed in my mind that are blocking me from a better life because Christ came that I might have life and have it more abundantly.[6]

I will overcome the invasion of mind monsters and live according to the assignment God has for me each day.

I will not conform any longer to the thinking pattern of this world, but I will be transformed by the renewing of my mind. I will retrain my mind with new and better habits.[7]

God has not given me a spirit of confusion. God is not the author of confusion.[8]

The Spirit God gave me does not make me timid, but gives me power, love, and self-discipline.[9]

I will partner with God and actively participate in becoming who He is calling me to be. I know God has good plans for me, plans to prosper me, not to harm me, plans to give me hope and a future.[10]

I will set my mind on things above, not on earthly things.[11]

Satan is a liar and the father of lies. There is no truth in him.[12]

My trust and confident hope will be fixed in Christ.[13]

I will not let my heart be troubled or afraid.[14]

I put my hope in the living God, who is the Savior of all men.[15]

I will not try to please men but God, who tests my heart.[16]

I live by faith, not by sight, and my faith does not rest on men's wisdom but on God's power.[17]

NOTES

INTRODUCTION

1. Natalie Wolchover, "How One Man Waged War Against Gravity," *Popular Science*, March 15, 2011, http://www.popsci .com/science/article/2011-03/gravitys-sworn-enemy-roger-babson -and-gravity-research-foundation (accessed September 26, 2011).

2. Ibid.

3. Ibid.

4. 2 Corinthians 10:5.

CHAPTER 1 · NEGATIVE INVADERS OF THE MIND

1. Matthew 1:19, emphasis added.

2. See Matthew 1:20–23.

3. Psalm 118:24.

4. Matthew 5:16.

CHAPTER 2 · F.A.I.T.H. IS THE EXTERMINATOR

1. Hebrews 11:1–2, The Message.

2. Exodus 3:11.

3. 1 Kings 3:5.

4. 1 Kings 3:7–9.

5. Acts 9:4–5.

6. Ed Reese, *The Life and Ministry of George Müeller,* Christian Hall of Fame Series no. 23 (Lansing, IL: Reese Publications, n.d.), http://www .believersweb.org/view.cfm?ID=177 (accessed September 26, 2011).

7. Patrick Fagan, PhD, "Why Religion Matters Even More: The Impact of Religious Practice on Social Stability," The Heritage Foundation, December 18, 2006, http://www.heritage .org/research/reports/2006/12/why-religion-matters-even-more -the-impact-of-religious-practice-on-social-stability (accessed November 10, 2011).

8. 2 Samuel 11:1.

9. 1 Corinthians 2:16.

10. Philippians 4:13, NKJV.

11. Isaiah 55:11.

12. Matthew 28:20.

13. Hebrews 11:1.

14. Philippians 4:19.

15. John 10:10, NKJV.

16. Galatians 3:7.

CHAPTER 3 · RECOGNIZING MIND MONSTERS

1. 2 Timothy 1:7.

2. 1 Corinthians 14:33.

3. Matthew 9:21.

4. Matthew 9:22.

5. Matthew 25:24–25.

6. Matthew 25: 27–28, 30.

7. James 3:3–5.

8. Matthew 12:34, ESV.

9. Ephesians 4:23.

CHAPTER 4 · REJECTING MIND MONSTERS

1. John Piper, *Amazing Grace in the Life of William Wilberforce* (Wheaton, IL: Crossway Books, 2006), 35.

2. Psalm 1:1–3, 6, AMP.

3. Mark 8:33.

4. See 2 Kings 22:16–20.

5. *Raising Helen*, directed by Garry Marshall (2004; Burbank, CA: Touchstone Home Entertainment, Buena Vista Home Entertainment), DVD.

6. Ibid.

7. Samuel Abt, "Cycling; With Paris Days Away, Armstrong Pours It On," *New York Times*, July 23, 2004, http://www.nytimes.com/2004/07/23/sports/cycling-with-paris-days-away-armstrong-pours-it-on.html (accessed September 29, 2011).

CHAPTER 5 · REPLACING MIND MONSTERS

1. Matthew 5, emphasis added.

2. 1 Corinthians 10:13.

3. As quoted by John Maxwell, *Thinking for a Change* (New York: Hachette Book Group, 2003).

4. Exodus 3:14.

5. Genesis 22:12–14.

6. Jeremiah 23:5–6.

7. Exodus 15:22–26.

8. Exodus 17:8–15.

9. Judges 6:24.

10. Jeremiah 10:12.

11. Proverbs 3:13–14.

12. James 1:5–8.

13. See Matthew 7:24–27.

CHAPTER 6 · RETRAINING YOUR MIND

1. James Riddett, "From Depressed to Happy in 11 Days," TheHabitGuide.com, http://www.habitguide.com/from-depressed -to-happy-in-11-days (accessed September 29, 2011); Roger Dobson, "It Takes 66 Days to Form a Habit," *The Telegraph*, July 18, 2009, http://www.telegraph. co.uk/health/healthnews/5857845/It-takes-66-days-to-form-a-habit.html (accessed October 1, 2011).

2. 2 Timothy 1:7, NKJV.

3. Bureau of Justice Statistics, "Total Correctional Population," http://bjs. ojp.usdoj.gov/index.cfm?ty=tp&tid=11 (accessed September 29, 2011).

4. Bureau of Justice Statistics, "Recidivism," http://bjs.ojp.usdoj .gov/index.cfm?ty=tp&tid=17 (accessed September 29, 2011).

5. Jacqui Goddard, "Florida's New Approach to Inmate Reform: A 'Faith-Based' Prison," *Christian Science Monitor*, December 24, 2003, http://www .csmonitor.com/2003/1224/p01s04-usju.html (accessed October 1, 2011); David Crary, "Faith-Based Prisons Multiply," Associated Press, October 13, 2007, http://www.usatoday.com/news/religion/2007-10-13-prisons _N.htm (accessed October 1, 2011).

6. Benjamin Franklin, *The Autobiography of Benjamin Franklin*, http:// www.gutenberg.org/cache/epub/1Ω48/pg148.txt (accessed September 29, 2011).

7. 2 Corinthians 5:17.

CHAPTER 7 · THE PERSON YOU WANT TO BE

1. Joshua Foer, "Secrets of a Mind-Gamer," *New York Times Magazine*, February 15, 2011, http://www.nytimes.com/interactive/2011/02/20/magazine/mind-secrets.html (accessed October 1, 2011).

APPENDIX B · DECLARATIONS TO CONQUER MIND MONSTERS

1. 1 Corinthians 2:16.

2. Philippians 4:8.

3. Psalm 119:11.

4. Proverbs 9:12.

5. Matthew 28:20; Philippians 4:19.

6. John 10:10.

7. Romans 12:2.

8. 1 Corinthians 14:33.

9. 2 Timothy 1:7.

10. Jeremiah 29:11.

11. Colossians 3:2.

12. John 8:44.

13. Hebrews 2:13.

14. John 14:27.

15. 1 Timothy 4:10.

16. 1 Thessalonians 2:4.

17. 1 Corinthians 2:5; 2 Corinthians 5:7.

Kevin Gerald lives to locate and communicate wisdom. He is the founder and pastor of Champions Centre in Tacoma and Bellevue, Washington, and author of several books, including *Forces That Form Your Future; Every Church Has a Culture; Pardon Me, I'm Prospering; The Proving Ground; Developing Confidence;* and *Raising Champion Children.*

Kevin also founded 1 Degree Mentorship Program for pastors and church leaders. The program is designed to give church staff and ministry teams practical wisdom that will help them lead more effectively in the local church and create a culture that makes people want to be part of their churches .

In addition to writing books and empowering leaders, Kevin is the executive publisher of *Champion Life Magazine*, a publication that aims to inspire, challenge, and equip readers to live a successful Christian life. His practical Bible teaching is also heard around the world through his television program, KevinGerald.tv.

For more information about Kevin's books and audio downloads, *Champion Life Magazine*, and 1 Degree Mentorship Program, visit www.championscentre.com or www.kevingerald.tv today!

FREE NEWSLETTERS
TO HELP EMPOWER YOUR LIFE

Why subscribe today?

- ❏ **DELIVERED DIRECTLY TO YOU.** All you have to do is open your inbox and read.

- ❏ **EXCLUSIVE CONTENT.** We cover the news overlooked by the mainstream press.

- ❏ **STAY CURRENT.** Find the latest court rulings, revivals, and cultural trends.

- ❏ **UPDATE OTHERS.** Easy to forward to friends and family with the click of your mouse.

CHOOSE THE E-NEWSLETTER THAT INTERESTS YOU MOST:

- • Christian news
- • Daily devotionals
- • Spiritual empowerment
- • And much, much more

SIGN UP AT: **http://freenewsletters.charismamag.com**

8178